THINK LIKE A STALKER AND STOP THEM

Michael Kenney

Private Investigator

Copyright © 2023 by Michael Kenney

All rights reserved. In accordance with the U.S. Copyright Act of 1976, the scanning, uploading, and electronic sharing of any part of this book without the permission of the publisher constitute unlawful piracy and theft of the author's intellectual property. If you would like to use material from this book (other than for the explicit purpose of review), prior written permission must be obtained. Reviewers may quote brief passages in reviews.

Printed in the United States of America

The advice found within this publication may not be suitable for every individual. This work is purchased with the understanding that neither the author nor the publisher is held responsible for any results. Neither author nor publisher assumes responsibility for errors, omissions, or contrary interpretations of the subject matter herein. Any perceived disparagement of an individual or organization is a misinterpretation.

Yes! We will find you!

DEDICATION

To those who tirelessly seek truth,
To the guardians of secrets and uncoverers of mysteries,
To the silent observers and tenacious pursuers,
This book is dedicated to you.

You are the seekers of hidden truths, the keepers of justice,
The ones who illuminate the shadows and expose deception.
With unwavering determination, you face the unknown,
Fearlessly venturing into uncharted territories of human nature.

To the sleepless nights spent sifting through clues,
To the relentless pursuit of facts and evidence,
To the moments of triumph and the setbacks faced,
This dedication is a tribute to your unwavering spirit.

And to the private investigators who stand in the shadows,
Silently observing, diligently gathering pieces of the puzzle,
Your dedication and commitment inspire.
This book is a testament to your invaluable contributions.

CONTENTS

	Acknowledgments	Pg # 1
Chapter One	Start Here	Pg # 4
Chapter Two	Stalkers Are Hurting	Pg # 11
Chapter Three	Stalkers Are Online	Pg # 19
Chapter Four	Use The Media	Pg # 24
Chapter Five	You Just Never Know	Pg # 29
Chapter Six	The New SSNs	Pg # 36
Chapter Seven	Early Interviews	Pg # 42
Chapter Eight	Think Like A Stalker	Pg # 45
Chapter Nine	Social Engineering	Pg # 51
Chapter Ten	Celeb Loves Her Phone	Pg # 55
Chapter Eleven	Social Media	Pg# 61
Chapter Twelve	Is Tech Good	Pg# 66
Chapter Thirteen	Pics and Calls	Pg# 74
Chapter Fourteen	Dating	Pg# 80
Chapter Fifteen	D.E.A.T.H.	Pg# 90
Chapter Sixteen	How To Stop The Stalking	Pg# 96

ACKNOWLEDGMENTS

I am deeply grateful to everyone who contributed to the realization of this book. In particular, I would like to express my special appreciation to the individuals who supported and inspired me throughout my career as a private investigator.

First and foremost, I extend my gratitude to the clients who entrusted me with their most sensitive and personal matters. Your faith in my abilities allowed me to delve into the intricate world of these cases. Without your cooperation, this book would not have been possible.

I would also like to acknowledge the unwavering support of my family and friends. Your encouragement, patience, and understanding during the long hours and countless nights I spent pursuing leads and analyzing evidence were invaluable. Your belief in my work gave me strength to persist in the face of adversity.

To my dedicated colleagues and fellow investigators, I am immensely grateful for your collaboration and camaraderie. Your expertise, professionalism, and shared passion for uncovering the truth have been instrumental in shaping my investigative skills.

I extend my appreciation to the legal professionals, law enforcement personnel, and forensic experts who have generously shared their knowledge and expertise with me. Your guidance and insights have been invaluable in navigating complex cases and ensuring the integrity of the evidence presented.

A special thank you goes to the authors, journalists, and researchers who have documented the world of investigations, both real and fictional. Your works have served as a source of inspiration, fueling my curiosity, and driving me to push the boundaries of my profession.

Finally, I would like to express my deepest gratitude to my mentors, whose wisdom and guidance have shaped me into the investigator I am today. Your support, trust, and belief in my abilities have been instrumental in my personal and professional growth.

To all those who have played a part, big or small, in my journey as a private investigator, please accept my heartfelt thanks. Your contributions have left an indelible mark on my life and have shaped the pages of this book.

> *"Reading every word is important to understanding and obtaining the details required to change your situation."*
>
> - *Michael Kenney*

If these chapters seem to vary in length or change topics sporadically, I would like to point out that it's intentional. My goal is to help you, concisely. Read every word, implement my suggestions, and your situation may change."

CHAPTER ONE

START HERE

"The first step towards getting somewhere is to decide you're not going to stay where you are."

- *JP Morgan*

First, I want to clarify that I am not trying to assist a stalker in any way, fashion or form. I work to stop the abuse daily, and I hope this book helps you or someone you know who is dealing with this situation.

Since signing nondisclosure agreements with many clients, I have changed the names, locations, and facts to protect privacy.

If you are in immediate danger, call 911. If you want to report an act of stalking to the National Center for Victims of Crime, call (855)484-2846.

If you think your cellphone has spyware, do the following and know that it works for both Apple IOS and Android:

Just like you are making a call, dial *#21#, this hit call.

A list will pop up, and everything listed should be <u>disabled</u>. If one listed is ENABLED, call your cellphone provider and report.

Let's get started with the first question I usually get: How did I become a private investigator? Well, my story is simple. While in college, my father recommended that I get a job to assist in paying for school and related expenses. He had a friend who ran a temporary agency. After a short period, I worked at an insurance company. I was soon hired directly and later became a claims adjuster. After graduation, I moved to Nashville, Tennessee, to pursue being a singer/songwriter. It did not take me long to decide I needed a paying job if I wanted to eat. I first sold printing in Nashville's industry area known as Music Row and performed other tasks. I made a lot of music contacts and friends, and this journey introduced me to an attorney and lifelong friend. This friend would play a critical part in my future!

After a few months, I decided to go back into insurance. Soon, I was working as a worker's compensation adjuster. Here, I hired my first round of private investigators to observe claimants to determine if their activities were within the doctor's orders. A couple of years later, I moved to a second insurance company where my files were tougher, and the environment was faster-paced. Here, I hired more investigators and stopped a ring of people defrauding the system on a much bigger scale. Ultimately, I was able to obtain a parking lot video of two carloads of people giving each other high fives before driving their fully insured cars into each other. The drivers and the passengers would then file lawsuits, hire the same attorney and chiropractor and attempt to settle for big dollars, except our video showed it was deliberate. After this, I was hooked!

At first, I asked our investigators if they would teach me or recommend books to educate me. All of them did not seem like they wanted to help me in my plight to do deeper investigations. Instead, they wanted me to hire them more! I finally started saying, "I have a case for you this weekend! The only catch is that I get to ride along." This period exposed me to different investigative tactics when my insurance job was losing its fun factor. I would call my dad frequently and complain about my job, and he would say, "Tell them to kiss your ass and start your own company." This advice pushed me in a new direction! Worker's Comp consulting! Wait what?

I gave my notice to the insurance company. And I was soon on my own, writing proposals for companies on how to save on their worker's compensation expenses and streamline their claims process. Companies loved the idea that I could show them how to save money and be smarter with off-work employees. I would stay up all night writing an amazing proposal only to have them compliment my work, delay me so they could test it out, and never hire me!

This left me thinking going out on my own was a huge mistake. After all, didn't entrepreneurs make big bucks right out of the gate? No! Luckily, I had stayed in contact with a friend who was the head of an investigative unit. He offered to hire my business to conduct light investigations. This work kept me afloat as I conducted interviews and drove long distances to take pictures and obtain public records.

When I got licensed by the state, everything changed. My old friends that were adjusters were kind enough to hire me, and business took off. I was getting videos and information that others were not. And, based on my own style, being nice and dumb! I will get into this strategy a lot more later in this book. One of the problems I faced when I hired investigators was that

I needed things they were not giving us, and they were giving us lots of items we did not need. This made my niche easy as I had a unique knowledge of what my former co-workers were looking for. I made their jobs a little easier and got better results.

So, there I am, in my new house on my new street, feeling larger than life, enjoying my cases, and making a difference! The suburb of Nashville where I lived offered great access to the interstate, and life was great! As an investigator that wanted to stay safe, I had chosen a dead-end street, and when they built the homes, they started at each end of the street. When they built my house, there was a span of address numbers. Think of it like this: at one end of the street, they started with house 123. At the end, 189, and in the middle, a gap of several possible addresses. So, guess what I did? I took the address numbers off my house and mailbox, requiring anyone looking for me to make an extra effort or take extra time looking. Thus, alerting me that there was a possible trouble person. Then it happened… one day, I was outside and saw a car pull up to my neighbor's house. The male asked my neighbor which house was mine. It was terrifying as my children were outside. My neighbor advised that I had recently moved (this was in relation to conversations I had incase this ever happened) out-of-state to California or Utah, or was it Maine? The problem male left discouraged, and I knew I needed a new solution. By the way, want to know how he found me in the first place? My publicly searchable state license had my home address!

The next day, I called my attorney friend on Music Row and told him what had happened. He reminded me he was also the building manager of a location in the heart of Nashville's entertainment business district. I then rented a room and had all my business mail delivered to this address. Then something unexpected happened…

Every Friday, I would stop by and pick up my mail. I would always hang around for an hour as I had moved to Nashville in the first place to be near the music scene. On these Fridays, I would meet people in my building, the buildings around ours, and the area. Whenever I met someone, the question would, "What do you do for a living?" would come up. When I would say, "I am a private investigator," they would almost always say, "You should talk to this person; they could use your help." And that is how I started working with celebrities. Yes, it was that simple and easy! The growth came when Nashville music executives and friends would move to Los Angeles or New York and take me with them in the form of a resource!

Within a few years, I had music artists, actors, industry leaders, managers, publicists, news outlets, and more calling me for advice and giving me interesting cases. I grew up in an industry that appreciated that I did not discuss their business with anyone. I was the silent information weapon that they needed and appreciated.

And that's how I started working on stalker cases!

You see, if you are well-known as a music star or an actor, some people believe they have a relationship with you. That they know you. They don't stop to think about the song that connects to them was penned by a songwriter or that the big movie role that was so meaningful was written by a team of writers. They actually don't know you at all, but this is America, and our celebrities are royalty.

DON'T MAKE IT EASY

I wanted to include some quick facts at the beginning of the book that could help someone being stalked ASAP. Since many murdered people were stalked first, take this seriously. Most stalkers are known by the person they are stalking; however, celebrities deal with their fame, and often, the stalker *thinks* they know them. In the case of celebrity, the stalker often falls in love with a character an actor is playing or thinks a music artist wrote a song that meant a lot to them. If you make it to Nashville, you'll see that songwriters are everywhere, and often, that meaningful song about love found was penned by three guys in ball caps drinking beer. Stalking and domestic violence seem to be a pattern for control and frequently are part of the same story. More women are stalked, but the number of men stalked is rising. The CDC performed a study and found that in the USA, one out of every six women has been stalked, and one out of nineteen men. However, it was not on their website at the time of this writing! I believe these numbers to be low as many people do not report it.

If you need help immediately, stop reading and call 911! Time is important, and catching a stalker on your property is better than telling the police about it later. Stalking should be a felony in every state in our developed country. Still, the fact is that only a few states take it that seriously. We hope this book helps you, your friend, family member, or anyone dealing with this terror.

Let's start with the obvious. If you're being stalked, let people know! Change your passwords and have your phone checked for spyware. Do not change your phone number but rather consider getting a second-line app! We may need those voicemails and texts for evidence. Add additional cameras at your residence. Stop driving the same route every day to work and eating at the same places. Make yourself the hardest one to be stalked. If you can afford to move, excellent. And STOP making contact or answering communications.

If you're dating someone and it is coming to an end, be direct when you break things off. Say, "I am not attracted to you and will never be." Did you know that murdered victims have been found with restraining orders on them? Often, women want to be nice and say, "I am not ready right now for a relationship." The stalker hears that you are not ready at this time but will come around at a future time. They are in pain, as it is sad for them to be broken up with. You've hit their self-worth and ego. In their mind, they often feel that they are the victim. The word *NO* really means "not right now." Our culture has movies, podcasts, songs, and TV shows about people being persistent in getting what they want. When you end things, end them with no doubt. No future contact; however, keep any messages (more on this later).

If you start getting harassed, do not communicate! If the stalker calls you 85 times and you answer on the 86th, they know it takes 86 attempts to talk to you. Think like a stalker. Trade vehicles with your friend, change your look and working hours, and be very aware of your surroundings. Contact the police, start a file they can reference, get an alarm system, etc. <u>And tell people!</u> If your office knows someone is a problem, they won't give them your new number or invite them to the Christmas party.

Remember, police don't wear bulletproof vests made of paper. Know that the restraining order is a step and not necessary a solution.

CHAPTER TWO

STALKERS ARE HURTING

"I have known people who radiate vulnerability. Their facial expressions say I am afraid of you. These people invite abuse. By expecting to be hurt, do they subtly encourage it?"

- *Ted Bundy*

What's worse? Knowing who the stalker is, or not knowing who they are?

This is something I have tried to determine over the years. Whether your stalker is an ex-lover or an admirer, both are bad and dangerous. Let's start with a little history and definition of a stalker.

The Department of Justice states on its website: "What is stalking? The term 'stalking' means engaging in the course of conduct directed at a specific person that would cause a reasonable person to fear for his or her safety or the safety of others or suffer substantial emotional distress."

They also recommend that if you are in immediate danger, you call 911. We hope you get the chance. They then recommend contacting your local police department to report stalking and stalking-related incidents and/or threats. This aligns with what I always say: the police are excellent at chalking around dead-bodies. Suppose your stalker is dangerous, and you see them. In that case, you may not have the opportunity to call your local police, who may take 20 minutes to arrive and not be trained to adequately address the situation. Remember the Jeffrey Dahmer bloody and naked victim that ran to the police only to be handed back to Dahmer to return to his house? I am not knocking the police in any way. I am only pointing out that every jurisdiction is not as astute as the L.A.P.D., N.Y.P.D., and Nashville's Metro Police. You can thank Orange County, California, for the more focused laws on Stalking, as they are making a difference.

Want to hear about a case where the names and locations have been changed? And how we solved it?

Enter Miss Singer. She is an award-winning artist who is smart and aware and has taken steps from past stalkers to avoid them. First, she drives an everyday car. You would never notice her sitting next to you in traffic and probably not even notice her standing in front of you at the grocery because she is aware and prepared. Here are how things progressed:

10/1 – receives a fan letter to her management praising her and thanking her for getting the stalker through a tough time. No return address and no name signed.

10/2 – receives another letter saying how beautiful she looked in a blue shirt and hat. This is the first red flag as the artist wore this to the gym; she determined later.

10/5 – receives a letter at her residence with a note that the stalker knows she likes flowers, yellow roses to be exact.

10/8 – receives a yellow rose in her mailbox at her residence. Not to worry, as she lives behind a gate and has security cameras. Security cameras that don't include a view of the mailbox.

10/15 – while she is at a local mall in her casual car, a note and a yellow rose are left on her windshield. This disturbs her, and I am hired. We then interview Miss Artist, who ultimately has no idea who it could be.

10/20 – a note arrives at her manager's office stating that her upcoming tour does not have a stop at a specific Florida beach stop. The stalker says he wanted to see her in her bathing suit on the beach while she was there. The stalker's language in this note is angrier. We all talk, and we formulate a specific plan.

10/25 – the artist leaves and heads back to the mall. The only difference is that we have a camera on the headrest this time to capture any activity. We were careful to hide the camera as sometimes the stalkers are very intelligent and suspicious. We will go as far as to say paranoid. Slam dunk, right? We even have a surveillance vehicle watching the car as well. Only nothing happens, no note, no flower, and no stalker.

10/27 – a letter arrives asking the artist why she hates the stalker and why she won't add the tour date. We search for people with related charges in the Florida town and note no good suspects.

10/29 – a letter arrives (please note that getting DNA and fingerprints off the letter is good for TV). This time, the letter says they are looking forward to seeing what the artist and her children will be wearing for Halloween. Everything changed with this note.

10/30 – we tail the artist everywhere she goes for the day: the mall, a restaurant, a gym, and a recording studio. We asked her not to look around, which she hated, and then it happened. An unknown vehicle was sitting near the studio with a guy that looked out of place. Since this was on Music Row and I walked it every day, I did not know the vehicle or the male.

We approached him and noted that he was solely focused on her exiting the car and entering the studio. We called her on the phone and asked her to come out and look into her trunk. By this time, we had run his license plate and had taken pictures of him that we had sent to the artist. Who was he? How did he know she would be at the studio since he did not follow her here? The artist then identified the man as an intern that had briefly worked for her. Later, we found out he was stalking her to upset her since he believed she had ruined his aspirations in the music industry. But wait, how did he know where she would be? We swept her vehicle looking for a tracker, looked at her phone for spyware, and examined everything we could think of. And then it hit me; let's interview her staff. And there it was, the artist had an assistant. The assistant was terrible about using the same password. The password was used on Google Calendar, which had the artist's entire daily schedule.

The same password had been given to the intern when he worked there to get access to a general fan Gmail. The same password was used for everything in the office and had even become a joke! And yes, the artist had listed on the calendar that she would go to the mall, gym, and everywhere else. That calendar was her life and almost cost it too. We backgrounded the ex-employee to find that he had past stalking charges and domestic violence. A simple background check could have saved a lot of pain and worry. Our stalker was encouraged to move back to Canada, and he has. We know this because we monitor him frequently.

This period disrupted the artist, who, luckily, went on to have more hits! This is just an example of what we will call stalking for revenge!

But wait...

So, I am a fan of the organization RAINN (Rape, Abuse, and Incest National Network). They add extra lines regarding stalking a little different than the DOJ:

"Stalking laws and definitions differ from state to state. Stalking behavior can take many forms, including:"

- Making threats against someone, or that person's family or friends

- Non-consensual communication, such as repeated phone calls, emails, text messages, and unwanted gifts

- Repeated physical or visual closeness, like waiting for someone to arrive at certain locations, following someone, or watching someone from a distance

- Any other behavior used to contact, harass, track, or threaten someone

Can you see why I like them? They do a better job of defining the problem.

Now, how about an example where the victim did know the stalker?

This case came from a concerned friend that would not leave me alone until I helped. The situation was that a female was new to town and went on a date, and the one-time "connection" via a dating app led to endless harassment.

Enter a beautiful 24-year-old girl who moved to town to get her career moving in the printing industry. Did you know that printing is Nashville's number one industry? It's true!

THINK LIKE A STALKER AND STOP THEM

So, after moving to the downtown area full of honky-tonks and tourists, she got lonely. As a result, she downloaded various dating apps and boom! She had multiple dates. The biggest difference was that she liked this mysterious tall fellow that treated her like a queen. He opened every door, paid for everything, and drove a nice car. So, that night, she and the guy we will call Mr. Car connected. The next morning all was great; he took her to breakfast and then asked to see her later. She was very happy, told her friends, and even posted about him on Instagram. The post caught the attention of her college ex-boyfriend, who called her. He was the love of her life, and she wanted to reconnect. A week later, the ex-boyfriend moved to town, and they were reunited. The problem was that Mr. Car had other future plans for her. He had told his mom, friends, and co-workers about this amazing girl and thought he had met his soul mate.

After repeated unreturned calls, Mr. Car decided to stop by her apartment and ran into her boyfriend. Things did not go well. Mr. Car threatened the boyfriend and called the girl many horrible names. He left in a rage, kicking her door as he departed the building.

The next day, the girl was called into her manager's office at work. They had received an anonymous call that she was doing drugs and lied on her application, including not actually graduating from college. This prompted the company to send her home while they investigated. Although she was later reinstated, it disrupted her life and caused her emotional problems.

The next day, she received a call from her father asking if she was ok. The father had just received a call stating that she had been arrested for drugs and was trying to raise money for bail. She advised her father that she was not.

Two weeks later, she noticed as she was out to lunch with friends that a man was walking up to her at a fast pace. It scared her, and she turned and noted that it was Mr. Car. He professed his love and asked her to reconsider. When she declined, he said he would call her boss and father again (identifying he was the troublemaker). And that he would go after anyone that "brought her joy." Later that evening, she looked out of her apartment window, and there he stood. The next week, every day, somewhere she went, he would be there, Standing and watching in silence. She assumed he was looking for dirt on her. When her father called and said someone had tried to get him fired from his job at a brokerage house, and her mother said someone had called the school where she worked, she knew it was getting out of control. When she called the police, she was told, "Well, he hasn't really hurt you yet, and most likely, he will just go away."

Enter us. After my friend had placed me in contact, we interviewed her. Mr. Car was showing up everywhere, following her, calling, texting, messaging, and pointing at her. It was time to turn the tables.

We located Mr. Car, who appeared to be well-put-together, articulate, and successful. We conducted a background check and determined that this was not the first time he had harassed a female over a broken relationship. We convinced our female client to get a restraining order. Only one catch; we wanted to give it to him.

Upon approaching him, we told him why we were there. He became irate. We told him about every time he had done this with dates, locations, names, and more. We added that we had been watching him for weeks, knew everything, had a video of what he was doing, and that it would become public in court. After we told him his address, social security number, date of birth, employer, and family members, he just stared at us. He was clearly most upset when we told him his mother's cell phone number and that we would text her copies of the restraining order. You see, an investigative technique in a background check is to say, "I'm going to find everything about you. Is there anything you want to tell me?" People will tell us things we would never have found!

He yelled, threatened us, and said, "She is not worth all this!" That was the last we heard from him because stalkers want to be the hunter, not the hunted! Be careful with this approach. We have been doing this for a long time, and this is best performed when someone has a good career, something to lose, and cares.

Many stalkers, again believing they are the victim, won't be working a job and believe the real victim ruined their lives. This is especially true in divorce cases when the father can't see his children. The direct approach can also backfire, so please remember to hire someone with experience.

CHAPTER THREE

STALKERS ARE ONLINE

"It is never too late to be wise."

- *Daniel DeFoe*

A stalker once told me, when caught and identified, that she could not have verified that a celebrity was home if not for the Amazon delivery when he answered the door! A package that *she* sent since you can add people and other addresses to your account. Convenient and clever.

Now, it was the month of June, and I got a call. "When is the next time you will be in Los Angeles?" I responded, "Friday," as I had meetings in Century City. And so it was on; a meeting between an A-list actor, his manager, attorney, publicist, and me. The topic: how in the "F" does this guy know so much about me?

Upon arrival, I noted that the celeb was wearing a hat, pulled down low, and sat in the corner of the dark restaurant. I thought, "Why are we meeting in a restaurant?" The answer was simple. Somehow, a man knew things about the celeb that no one knew. The meeting started with questions like can people listen through my phone? Yes. Can people monitor my every move? Yes. Can you make me feel safe in my own home again? Yes.

Somehow a male would text the actor telling him what he was wearing and had detailed information about him. He knew about vacations, the girls he was dating, and what times he was coming and going from his residence. But how? We conducted our normal interview and learned more than we wanted to about this person. We then visited his house. Within a few minutes, he (the A-list actor) got a text asking who the people out by his pool were. Recently, the secret stalker had stated he wanted money to stop the harassment or would put everything he had online for the world to see. I decided we all should exit and go to a coffee place down the street. I kept asking, "What is he saying now?" We quickly noted that the male's information was limited. Although frightening, it seemed to boil down to the actor's home, pictures not on social media, and knowledge of things he had purchased online.

I will be the first to tell you that some smart con artists are out there! After interviewing the actor for over an hour, the information came out. And how did the secret stalker do it?

One day, the actor got an email (everyone's information has been leaked multiple times in data breaches and sold on the dark web repeatedly. Your phone number, email, DOB, address, etc.). The email stated that his giant online retailer account had been hacked and to call the below toll-free number immediately. There are many versions of his scam, but the male knew from seeing the actor's house and cars that our actor had money. The actor called the number and was told $7,500 in laptops and other items had been purchased on his account. And that they needed to confirm they were legit purchases. Of course, they were not. Now comes the scam: the male, knowing the actor's email he acquired in a data breach, went to the online retailer's website, put in the email, and hit *lost password*. They then told the actor that they (the retailer) had sent him a confirmation and needed the six-digit code. Since the actor thought he was talking to the retailer, he gave it to them, granting them access to his full account. They confirmed his most recent purchases since they were granted access and gained his trust. They told him they would deny the charges and asked him for the (past) password he was using. He, of course, gave it to them. To reverse everything, he would need to change his password and then change it back to the original password so he could confirm to them that it was indeed him they were talking to. Following this? So now they had access to all his past purchases and photo backups, and since he was lazy with the passwords, they had access to his doorbell camera. Problem solved. But only one problem: they were in India!

We had him change his passwords and contacted an organization assisting in scams from that area. Everything stopped when we obtained pictures of the secret stalker scammer via social media and sent them to him, threatening to tell his parents and authorities. This blew his mind, and he stopped. He deleted all items he had; to date, we have not seen a single item made public. There is something about telling a secret stalker their name and home address that gets their attention! In this case, it was the fear of his parents knowing that worked.

This also leads us to an old adage, "Beware of gifts!" Think of the Trojan Horse.

What's the easiest way someone can plant a bug? Give it as a gift, of course.

The problem with listening and spy camera devices, a.k.a. bugs, is that they need a power source. If they are battery-operated, then the stalker needs continuous access to them to change the battery. If it plugs into power, the problem is solved. So, since the Giant retailers sell everything from phone chargers with hidden cameras to tracking devices, obtaining these devices are easy.

So, think about it: a stalker can order a car tracker, a phone charger with a hidden camera; their own cellular trail camera to place facing your house that can live stream. Then google your address to get a layout of your neighborhood, yard, and maybe even your vehicles shown in the driveway. This is not to mention the members in your household, their ages, and a link to their social media and LinkedIn to acquire an employer. But wait, at least those purchases can be tracked, right? Sure, but who is monitoring until after the stalking incident, and what if they order off sites like Wish.com or Temu? Remember, we are not here to educate the stalker; saying this helps our fight by educating you!

So, all of the above is to share a story that happened a couple of years ago. A client of ours was going through a divorce, and her abusive husband wanted custody of their two kids. One day, she received a package for her birthday with a card featuring a scribbled signature that looked like her uncle's and was mailed from his town two hours away. She opened the package to find a new phone cube charger, a phone power cord, a car charger, and a USB drive in the shape of her favorite cartoon character. A nice gift for a nice person. After a couple of months, she was served with papers stating she was not permitted to have a boyfriend stay the night when her kids were present. That she had drunk too much wine on one occasion when the kids were home (they were asleep) and was planning to move out of the state.

I was hired to determine how the ex knew any of this. Beware of gifts! First, we set up cameras for his visit when he picked up the kids. As soon as she left the room, he walked over to the kitchen and replaced the phone charger with an identical one. Once he left, we used a camera detector that could spot cameras via the light they emit. Inside the charger was a mini SD card for recording audio and video. We then asked where she received the charger, and she responded that it was from her uncle. Upon calling her uncle, he admitted that he had forgotten her birthday and apologized. We then examined the character USB drive. It was a spy device that would copy and transmit after downloading malware to her computer. The screenshots it took and transmitted included emails, surfing history, and questionable online behaviors. Luckily, the car charger tracker didn't work. The phone charging cord was a device to swipe information; however, it was not set up properly and did not benefit his efforts.

The USB drive and the single camera cost her custody for a short time. The information was damaging, and she told the truth about drinking the wine and the violation by having a boyfriend spend the night. The ex, of course, lied that he sent the gifts; however, we could prove that he ordered the phone charger from a local spy store (yes, they have cameras too). The gifts caused her great grief and anguish, and to this day, she will not accept any gifts of an electronic nature. On a side note, it was fun to watch him deny buying the items until we showed the video from the store.

CHAPTER FOUR

USE THE MEDIA

"Whoever controls the media, controls the mind."

- *Jim Morrison*

I work with a lot of musicians, both the pros and the up-and-comers. I often hear in a conversation that they are concerned that they will get denied a loan at the bank. I tell them the bank needs new customers to create new loans and increase deposits. This seems to give them some peace and make the journey a little less scary.

You see, the media is the same way. They need new news stories and lots of various content, and they love a scoop! Let me repeat: they need content to have top stories and demand the highest advertising dollars. That said, I have primarily stayed out of the media. I frequently work behind the scenes to assist, and I don't have an ego when it comes to taking credit. If it helps someone in need, I try to help.

One day, I got a call from a top female music executive. She was having some weird things happening at her rural residence and constantly felt like she was being watched. I visited her large home on many acres and noted that overall, her cameras would pick up any movement. As I entered the home, she had an alarm system, a dog, and large windows.

Her story began with, "I was dating this guy… we met when I took my mother to a repair shop, and we just hit it off. He was kind, good looking and told me he was ex-military and would love to take me out. Since he was good to my mom and funny, I accepted." Ok, this was where I started asking more and more questions. She further said they dated for a few months, and then she thought he was just weird. She broke things off, and he did not take it well. The next few months, she would hear sounds out at her tree line, see shadows passing her front door, and see what appeared to be a head ducking down when she looked out one of the huge windows. She lived alone but had friends join her frequently for cookouts and more. Did we mention that her dog was frequently barking at these activities and more?

Then one night, she was having friends over, and as a guy friend left, he noted that his tires were flat. They could not figure out how he got four flat tires until they noticed they had been cut. They entered the house and watched her cameras; nothing was captured on video. They could see the car, but not much was happening around it. She had her friend spend the night and dealt with the tires the next day.

All was good for a while until she had another male friend visit, and his tires were slashed again. Again, the cameras were not beneficial. The male stayed the night, only this time, sounds outside scared them both, the dog barked, and no visible activity was noted. The next morning, one of her tires was cut too.

Since the third time is the charm, she had a large party later that month and only the people that stayed after midnight had a tire slashed. Cameras were rolling but did not trigger in the darkness.

So, as she and I stood at her front door, I started looking at her camera positions. I walked her property and found a small road pull-off about a mile down the road and fresh tire tracks as if someone had recently parked there. We installed some additional cameras to catch the blind spots, and what we caught would have unsettled anyone. That night around midnight, our night vision camera caught a male crawling on his belly slowly and deliberately up the driveway. A very long driveway. And he was carrying something. As he got closer, we could tell that it was a huge knife, and as he arrived next to her vehicle, he slowly, very slowly, cut into the tire. It was truly scary. Guess who it was? So, the next day, we had the local authorities look at the video in her small rural suburb. They agreed it was unusual, but unless they caught him in the act, there was not much they could do. A phone call to the man was only received with "It wasn't me. I was not in town" excuses. He was honestly so convincing we had to rewatch the video. But remember, he had training for this kind of thing. Since he had been to the residence many times, he would have studied the camera locations and known the blind spots and her dog. And the big question, would he get bored cutting tires and come after her?

I contacted a reporter I knew and respected and sent him the video. He was blown away too. The green tint of the night vision, his slow crawling, giant reflecting knife, and reflecting eyes would make anyone move out of their house that night. He agreed to do the story; the music executive as fantastic on the segment. When the segment aired, people were outraged.

Women came to her defense, and most importantly, the man was getting a lot of heat.

He received so much flack that he was nowhere to be found when they wanted to do a follow-up segment. The employer told us that he had packed up and moved the night the segment aired. We performed a skip trace to locate him, and he had moved far, far away! Sometimes the media can get the needed exposure and is one tool in the fight against stalkers!

Media and Elections!

Los Angeles county is big! So, when an attorney called me and told me about one of his clients being threatened and hiding there, I did not worry. The female had long dated a man and had a child with him. He had tried to hurt her and the child; the last time he found her, she had a hospital stay for over a week. She feared for her life, and he told her frequently that if he could not have her, no one could.

Hence, she moved frequently, staying with friends, family, and coworkers. She drove a friend's car, stayed off social media, and ensured her child was home-schooled. Her job was in a large building with security, a gated parking garage, and cameras. She once told me that her work was the only place she felt secure.

It is important to note that she had a restraining order and that he had been arrested several times for stalking her. He did not care; he was getting worse with his son's birthday approaching. Somehow, every time he would eventually find her location. She used a prepaid cell phone (burner phone), which was not a smart phone. She was hypervigilant about her surroundings, had cameras, and frequently changed her appearance. She was one of the best I had met. Each time he would find her, it was worse. If someone stepped in to help, they were punished, too, and even her attorney was frightened after being threatened multiple times.

We assisted in what I will call a "drop house." A rental with a garage that you pull up to, and the door goes up. You drive into the garage, and the door goes down. No real contact with anyone around you. The rental includes all utilities and is located on a dead-end street, making it easy to spot visitors. This is important because you can be tracked via your utilities if they are in your name. She wanted to move out of the area altogether, but the court dates and her family were in the area.

The "drop house" worked like a charm; she felt secure and could see anyone that entered the street. She said this was one of the best times in this dark period. Then one day, she opened her garage and backed out. As she stopped at the end of her driveway, her neighbor was being interviewed by the news about a project in the area. And there she was, on camera in the background. She exited the area, and when she arrived at work, she started crying after realizing she had made no effort to look different that day as she was running late. She called her next-door neighbor, who was watching her son, and put them on alert.

If you are wondering why she didn't send a huge guy to threaten the ex, she did. On multiple occasions and the outcome was the same. The big guys got hurt. And for a "hurting stalker," this approach does not work. We went to work when we got the call that the news had her in a shot. What station, which reporter, etc.? Since all the reporters have social media, it is relatively easy to reach them, but getting a response is another matter. So, now you're thinking the ex showed up at the house? No, the reported talked to us after we stopped by the station. It turned out that it was not a live shot and that they were willing to use a different interview for the segment. And the best part? They wanted to tell her story and could not believe that the ex could behave this way and keep getting out of jail.

A week later, a story aired about the failures of how these cases were handled. As you may or may not know, judges are elected. And elected officials don't like bad publicity. Not only did her ex face many more consequences the next time there was an issue (he tried to enter her work), but the story also helped many people in the same situation. The media came through and made a difference in many lives. On a side note, the ex is now in prison after striking an authority figure.

CHAPTER FIVE

YOU JUST NEVER KNOW

"To expect the unexpected shows a thoroughly modern intellect."

- *Oscar Wilde*

Currently, I have seven death threats. I have many more, but seven where I think the person is capable. Sometimes in the world, a celebrity is being nice or charitable, and the other person thinks, *BAM! We are in love.* This is the case of one medical professional I greatly fear to this day.

During a stadium show, a musical artist hurt their hand and went to get medical attention after the show. While at the medical facility, they were assisted by a doctor who, by chance, was a big fan. He asked the artist as many questions about where they lived, what they drove, and who they were dating as they did about the injury. He held her hand much too long for her liking and told her she had beautiful eyes. The artist was patched up and out the door but felt the doctor lingered too long with them and, after asking for a photo, was a little creeped out.

A few days later, the artist was home, and waiting for her were flowers, a box of her favorite expensive treats, and a note from the good doctor saying how nice it was to meet her. The note also mentioned he wanted to follow up with her about her hand and offered to drive a couple of hours to check on her. The artist ignored the gifts and offer, followed up with her doctor, and was fine. How did he get her home address? She wrote it on the medical form (a violation of HIPAA).

The next weekend, she was performing at a show, and the good doctor was standing in the front row. We later estimated that he had paid a small fortune from a scalper for this seat and was by himself. After the show, security refused to let him backstage until he said he was the artist's friend and had treated her as her doctor. He proceeded to show them his medical credentials. And after security spoke with the artist, he was permitted to enter the backstage area. On seeing her, he hugged her and asked if she had received the gifts? She replied yes, and he said the next step was grabbing a drink or dinner. When the artist stated that she was not interested in a relationship, the good doctor smiled and said it was every woman's dream to be married to a doctor! Married?! She ignored this and politely made her way to her tour bus. The good doctor stood there for an extended period, then turned to her tour manager and said he would marry her someday.

The next day, the artist received a call from the doctor, and when she did not answer, she received a text asking when they were getting together. She ignored the text and calls until she finally blocked him. He then started calling from various numbers to get her to answer. She had her attorney write him a letter, which only made the doctor angry. He wrote to her again, saying, "We are meant to be together," and she ignored him more. After the harassment didn't stop, legal papers were filed, and the medical board was notified. It still did not stop. When he showed up at her house one night, the cameras were enough to finally get the needed attention. After it was determined that he acquired her cell phone number from her medical chart, it was noted as another violation of the law. After what we will call a light slap on the doctor's hand, he was released. A couple of weeks later, he started driving a couple of hours frequently to her house and sitting down the street. Then it was cat and mouse. They would see his car and call the police. He would leave the area and return an hour later, and the police would never see him. This occurred over and over. He also watched her tour schedule. If she was off the road, he was down the street, hoping for a chance to meet.

After hearing her story and exiting a restaurant, she could point across the street to a car. His car. With him in it. As I started to walk towards the vehicle, it sped away. The license plate came back to him, of course. This last segment led to a protection order that would not allow him within 100 yards. And the harassment stopped for a period.

A few weeks later, a music magazine posted online that she was back in the studio. A quick google search would provide the name of her producer, the studio she normally recorded, and a map of the area.

Since he had not bothered her in a few weeks, it appeared all was well. I was working in my office late one night when I got a call from her producer. His car was parked down the street, and they were certain he would leave if they called the police, as it was suspected that he had a police scanner. It was cold out, and he was just sitting there staring at the studio. I called a friend at the local PD and gave him the information. Then I drove to a nearby parking lot and watched the good doctor until the authorities arrived. The doctor just stared at the studio doors. Two police cars, my friend and I all approached the good doctor simultaneously. He exited the vehicle without incident. When asked why he was there, he stated he was waiting on his girlfriend to get out of the studio, and then they were heading to dinner (he had even made reservations). On his front passenger seat, under a coat, was a gun, a police scanner, towels, rope, and some chemicals in an unmarked bottle.

He was charged and ultimately is not practicing anymore. And guess who he vowed he would get even with for ruining his life? ME. Not his behavior or actions but the person he believed caused his pain. He has now moved to a different town and is working a non-medical job. I keep tabs on him as I know he wants to get even to this day.

The artist has since married and is forever grateful for our efforts. She is more aware than ever that she must be nice to people but with a smart, reserved eye. She later told me that she had nightmares every night during this period as she thought he was everywhere she went. She thought she saw him everywhere and at every tour stop, coffee shop, and hospital she passed.

Refrigerator Tells ALL

We have a long-time client who has dealt with many stalkers. She has overcome their tactics, and we are always there to assist. When COVID-19 hit, stalkers knew celebrities would be home in one place, and we saw a big increase in harassment. As an influencer, she was constantly posting about what she was doing; however, per our advice, not in real-time. If she posted she was at the beach, we knew she had been there days before. This is an excellent lesson and makes it more difficult to see your posting locations if they are not from moments ago.

A brand approached our client and offered her $40,000 to post in her kitchen with their product on the counter behind her. This is a frequent strategy for fans to think the influencer must use the product. Since this celebrity has multiple houses, shooting in the kitchen was not a big deal. The problem is that stalkers spend a lot of time studying their victims in the celebrity world. They have looked at sites like Realtor.com for inside pictures of all their houses. They study which pool is at which home, etc. The client shot a quick video when the brand requested a last-minute post before an event. However, in her rush, she did not notice that her refrigerator LED screen was visible and popped up an alert.

The screen alert said:

The Date / Weather

Vacation tomorrow!!!

FLT at 8:00AM

Hangar #12

XOXOXOXOX!!!!!!!

This gave Mr. X the opportunity he was looking for. After about 10 minutes, she realized her mistake and took the post down. She reposted without the refrigerator in the background, and all was good. Mr. X, however, had taken a screenshot of the original post and now had her plans for the next day and was driving to her place shortly after. He had been studying her residences and kitchens. He knew that the granite countertop, the island lights, and the window position meant she was in Long Island. Since the picture of her alert included the date, he knew right where she was. But wait, how could he be following her on social media since he was blocked? Because he had created multiple fake accounts and watched all her posts. Stalkers are driven and adapt.

Did we mention we knew exactly who the stalker was? He was a frequent menace that we would call Mr. X from the block. Mr. X was an ex-boyfriend before her fame began and was an abusive big man with a huge temper. They had been high school sweethearts, and she had left him because of the physical and mental abuse. He was scary and got worse over the years after the breakup.

She stayed in the house that night. When the driving service did not arrive to pick her up for her flight, she tried to call them, but her cell phone had no coverage.

She decided to walk next door to her neighbor's house to ask for help; it is important to note that she was not alarmed. It was early, but the neighbor was usually up for their morning run. As she got to the bottom of her driveway, there he was. Mr. X was standing there inside her fence. He asked, "Did you really think I would not find you?" She was horrified. She yelled to the neighbor, but no one heard her. She told us later that she felt alone and was certain he would kill her.

She decided to take a chance and played up to Mr. X. She talked about the old days, the old neighborhood, teachers, and his mom. She talked about how his grandmother took him to church on Sundays and would be disappointed with him. After a few minutes of feeling like a hostage in her own home, she recalled that I had given her a special device the previous year. Since her WiFi and cell were not connecting and she did not have a landline phone, she was concerned. She said it was horrifying to think that her home alarm system used a cell line to connect with their service. The device I gave her was a backup; she thought talking to her neighbors about it was a pain. The device was a simple switch that activated blinking lights around the outside of the house to alert people that she was in distress. I might add that she fought me on this in the past, but since she had had previous stalkers and often lived alone, it made sense. After about 10 minutes, she saw her neighbor looking up the driveway and driving away. A few minutes later, the police arrived, and Mr. X ran away from the property. When captured, Mr. X had a cell phone blocker (an illegal device that blocks cell connections), a WiFi blocker (illegal), and a screenshot of her post on his phone. Where did he buy these blocking items? Chinese websites!

He was arrested and booked and is away for an extended period due to some other issues. He was patient, but she was ready. In these days of advanced technology, it is always smart to think of simple old-school ways to communicate that you require help.

CHAPTER SIX

THE NEW SSNS

"What's dangerous is not to evolve."

- *Jeff Bezos*

It's simple; you're checking out at the grocery store, and there it is: *Please enter your phone number for extra savings*. Outside of their information-gathering tactics lies a security problem. Since most people no longer have landlines, they put in their cell phone numbers. Seems simple and easy, and you can use your cell number for all the discounts from the oil change place to your favorite store. If you are dealing with a stalker, beware of using your real number.

Apps like WhatsApp, Second Phone Number, Phoner, and many more, offer an extra phone number (Google does too. But don't they know enough about you already?). WhatsApp is good if you don't have cell coverage and need to make a call over WiFi. The real bonus is that you can use the second number for all the collection data points, like the grocery.

Here is one of our tactics when looking for someone who does not want to be found. We once found a man we were told could not be found (never tell me this) by giving HIS cell phone number at a car dealership. We needed to serve him papers regarding a lawsuit. It was easy; he drove a specific high-end car, and only one dealership was in the area. We told the dealer we were selling the car and needed all the maintenance records. They gave them to us. In the printout was the last work performed on the car in another state. We then called that dealer to get a reminder of when the next appointment was, and we were told in three weeks, on a Monday. The car was scheduled to have an oil change and the tires rotated. We waited three weeks, traveled to the state, and at 8:00AM, we served him as he arrived at the dealership. He begged me to know how I found him. I simply replied, "You need friends that don't talk." I am sure he spent the rest of the day questioning his friendships! Our client was happy, the lawsuit proceeded, and the wronged people felt they received justice. But this made me question how cell phone numbers are like our social security numbers. Outside of tracking a cell phone, knowing just the number can help you get a lot of information. We used to call the local pizza place, give the number of who we were looking for, and ask for the last address where they made a delivery! Protect your number and use an alternative number for data collection points. Now comes the story about Alice!

Our client called us, crying about dealing with an ex-husband who could always find her. She was an actor in some minor roles, and her agent was a good friend of mine. She had custody of her son. And due to the ex's drug addiction and physical abuse, he had lost custody and was not permitted contact (he also had six DUIs). She did not have the means to keep moving, so she reached out to me at a seminar explaining that I knew her agent. Before you think I'm the most wonderful guy in the world, she lived near a Whataburger, and I was craving some spicy ketchup!

I sat down and interviewed her, going over my checklist. "What is your day job, social media, the organizations you're in, and the church you attend?" I asked all of this to acquire a pattern. She would change all the above every time he caught up to her. As he sold drugs, he had free time and the means to jump on a plane and arrive at her newest location. We ran a scan on her cell phone to determine if it was hacked, and no, it was not. She changed emails and had the utilities in a friend's name. And then it came out. She had a favorite store that she frequented, which was a condition of hers when moving to a new place. It had to have this store in the area! We went together to the store and asked to see her purchase history. We were declined! We waited and asked another worker and were again declined. Then we waited for a third worker who told us how to access it online. So, we did, and when it asked for her cell number, we performed a *lost password* (he had set up the online account).

There on the screen was her purchase history with times, dates, locations, and amounts. Mystery solved. Only we took it another step: we changed her cell number, and I had fellow investigators across the nation use her cell at the checkout and make small purchases. I am sure he traveled quite a bit before figuring this out. You see, once he knew her store location, he would travel there and wait. Once, he waited for five days for her to come by, so he could follow her home. She is now safe, and all is good until her son starts school, as we will need specific instructions given to the school not to place online that he is in the honor role, on a sports team, etc.

BEWARE OF TEXT LINKS

Recently, I received a call from an actor that was literally on my TV as he called. I thought this was crazy and made a small joke about his role. He asked me to get to NYC the next day as he was panicked. He had received an email that an anonymous stalker knew all of his passwords (they listed two of his logins) and his location and was about to ruin his life if they were not paid. I caught a later flight out of Nashville and arrived at his apartment. First, this person is suspicious of everyone and paranoid about everything. He once called me in the middle of the night because he thought a taxicab was beeping in a special pattern to communicate that he had just arrived home.

We went through the checklist and ultimately decided to check his phone for malware. And there it was. His phone had been hacked, transmitting everything he did: banking, pictures, text, emails, etc. They had access to anything they wanted. I asked him the tough question, "Have you been browsing porn sites on your phone?" He answered, "No." Some sites in that space have tracking software, so it was a good question. When asked when this started, he knew the approximate time a couple of days before. I studied his phone and reviewed every app, email, and text message. Then there it was. He had received a text with a link that read, "Updated schedule." He did not know the number it came from and said it was a mistake as there was nothing there when he clicked it. Yes, there was! It was a virus. Lucky for him, they did not know he was a celebrity.

We spent the rest of the night changing passwords and setting monitoring for his banking. The problem with these text viruses is that they can take over your phone, infect your computer when connected, and be passed to your contacts. Then they can send the same messages like it's coming from you. He ultimately decided to head to Verizon in the morning and replace the phone. Beware when you do this, as simply transferring the information off your phone to the new phone can also transfer the virus. The key here is that we caught it fast before they could use his information against him and demand payment to unlock the phone. This is becoming a serious problem.

THINK LIKE A STALKER AND STOP THEM

A TACTIC TO STOP THE STALKING

Like many of my calls, this one came late a night. A star singer dealing with a stalker that would show up everywhere he went. He went to the grocery, and she was there. He went to the movies, and she was there. You get the picture. One night, he decided to go to his 24-hour gym. At around 2:00AM, he departed and decided to stop at a local gas station to get his favorite water. And there she was, restraining order and all, standing to the side of the gas station, smiling at him just out of view of the cameras.

Since she had threatened him but never seemed to get into trouble, he was reluctant to call the police again. And the police would ask him if he was seriously scared of her. Then act like that was ridiculous. In his call, he stated he could not do this anymore: reporting her, her getting arrested, denying she was doing anything, and then being free to leave. Being pretty has its advantages. He could get a restraining order only after she was caught on his property with a gun. He was fed up, and yes, he had dated her for a time. So, he asked me how to stop this once and for all. I asked where he was at that moment, and he informed me he was on I-65 just South of Nashville. I told him to drive to Alabama, and I would have some people waiting for him at a particular exit. Since stalking over state lines is considered a felony, this tactic worked. He arrived at the location, and she was arrested when she pulled in behind him. Only this time, it stuck. She won't be threatening him for some time now. This is a lesson in using the law. In 1996, President Clinton signed into law the Interstate Stalking Act, which makes it a felony to cross state lines with the intent to harm. This also applies to the internet and U.S. Mail; however, it seems undeniable when standing over the state line.

HELP THE POLICE

If you or someone you know is a victim of stalking, plan on doing most of the police work yourself. We have included a form in this book that you are welcome to use to document all activities. The first knee-jerk reaction is often to delete a person's texts or emails, but please don't. You will be building a case of harassment with dates, times, locations, and witnesses and noting cameras in the area that can document the situation. Make sure you are always prepared. We recommend taking a self-defense class and making friends with the police. An easy way to do this is by visiting a substation, like in a mall. If the officers at that location are aware you have an issue and the stalker shows up, you have the upper hand.

Instead of deleting your phone number, get a second number app and use this with everyone but the stalker. If you simply change your number, they will almost always find it anyway. If you are a female, have a female friend redo your voicemail, as sometimes the male stalker is triggered by your voice. You may think a male voice will scare your stalker, but it usually just makes them want to learn more information. If you are a male, have a friend do your voicemail too. Have it short and simple. Eventually, your original number will have a lot of evidence to assist you.

CHAPTER SEVEN

EARLY INTERVIEWS

"Life is a succession of lessons which must be lived to be understood."

- *Ralph Waldo Emerson*

Guess when a celebrity tells the most about themselves? In the earliest interviews of their career. They often say their real name, where they are from, where their favorite restaurant is located, and what they love to do for hobbies. You get the idea. With sites like YouTube, the information is everywhere. So, here is a tale of saying too much before your publicist requires that you take media training and stop sharing as much information!

I love movies. They say never meet your heroes; however, I have to say that some actors are pretty wonderful people. When "spiders" crawl the web looking for information, the information ends up on search engines. I like the site DogPile.com as it searches several search engines at once. One particular search provided a link to an actor when he was just getting started in the business. This early interview would prove to be a problem.

It started with a girl that knew he was married and didn't care. She also worked in the industry and seemed to be part of many of his projects. They started the affair at a wrap party when filming was completed. When he broke things off, she was out for blood. It first began with the girl calling his wife. After a lot of counseling, he and his wife worked things out. This upset the girl, and she started working to destroy his marriage.

An old interview provided that when he was home in, we will say, anywhere in town U.S.A., he would always visit his uncle's pub, "The Rusty Frog with Red Hat on a Bike." When he went home for a fast visit and posted it, the girl texted the wife from a burner number. She said her name was Jasmine and that she had hooked up with her husband after he visited the pub. This sent the wife into a rage. When the actor went to New York for a premiere, the wife received a call that he was at a strip club and took the stripper back to a specific hotel (he stated in the early interview that he loved a certain brand because of their soap). The girl seemed to try to ruin him whenever he was away from his wife.

When an email arrived in the wife's inbox one day from his manager stating that he knew the actor was having an affair with his current co-star, it became too much.

He called me and asked for help. The manager said he did not send the email and had no idea how this happened. One thing that helped at this segment was that when we reviewed the email, you could tell it was not written by a man. Yes, men and women write differently! First, we acquired videos from the pub, the hotel, and various other places, and lucky for him, his wife believed the proof. We then found the craziest part: on the manager's login page was an entry that the girl had made when she visited his office late on a Friday after he had left for the weekend. It was assumed she snuck into his office and used his open computer to send the email.

Sometimes the past, good or bad, can haunt you. On a happy note, the couple is still together, and the last time he needed anything from me was to background-check his new male assistant. The girl, however, has an upcoming court date for cyber issues that will stick.

CHAPTER EIGHT

THINK LIKE A STALKER

"Know thy self, know thy enemy. A thousand battles, a thousand victories."

- *Sun Tzu*

I love reverse engineering. I like the idea of taking something apart to examine it and determine how it works. Thinking like a stalker will improve your security and make you safer.

Let's start with your residence. If you don't have cameras, get them. Now, step outside and monitor what the cameras are recording. Where are the blind spots, where can you stand and not be seen, and can the camera wires be cut? If so, get wireless cameras or conceal the wires immediately! Do you need a ladder to reach the cameras? If not, place them higher.

First, start with camera placement. If your cameras have blind spots, get more cameras. Ring cameras can be charged and placed anywhere and offer motion detection. Trail cameras are great for seeing your whole property (within reason) and can be live-streamed. Have eyes on every part around your property. The stalker is going to notice cameras and avoid them. If you have this in mind, you can lure them into a dark area, maybe next to a shed, and get an amazing video to document your case. If they look in your window and think they are invisible to your cameras, your new camera will capture them for proof. And once confronted, they will most likely avoid the residence, fearing you have more cameras.

Cameras = evidence = deterrent.

I often hear people recommend getting a dog. In many instances, I feel like this is a great early alert system. However, we have had cases where the dog obviously knew the stalker and didn't bark or alert at all. Plus, your dog can't tell the police that someone stood behind your tree for four hours.

Motion flood lights to illuminate your entire property are good too. Someone creeping along the side of your house does not like being revealed. We have had neighbors complain about these in the past. However, they usually understand once you tell them why you have them.

Plant painful thorny plants below your windows so that anyone trying to peek regrets it. We don't recommend this; however, we know people that have placed other things under their windows to stop peepers, too, including a bear trap. I said we don't recommend it!

Have a different security company sign visible than the one you really use. Let the stalker spend hours learning about the system they think you have, only to be wrong. This is an excellent tactic; once they are wrong about you in one area, they may have to rethink other areas.

Talk to your friends, coworkers, and neighbors to be your extra set of eyes. Neighbors can alert you to a car down the street or parked in the nearby church. Coworkers will know when someone should not be present at your job. And friends will offer to drive you home, have you stay at their place, trade cars with you, etc. I will say this again: <u>tell someone</u>. We dealt with a situation where an ex-husband pulled up on our client while she was taking the trash out. The alert neighbors knew he shouldn't be there, and our client had left her phone inside. The neighbor called the police and started yelling that the police were on the way. The ex-husband later denied having been there and had his dad say they were golfing together. The problem was that two neighbors and our client all had video of him first sitting down the street (he knew it was trash day) and then trying to abduct her. This documentation was crucial to her winning custody.

Do not drive the same way to and from work every day. Let's repeat: do not drive the same way to and from work daily! Mixing up your routes and times will make it more difficult to determine your schedule.

Do not get coffee every day at the same place at the same time. Have a friend go or, better yet, change the times and go to different places. This applies to restaurants, bars, churches, and any pattern that can be established.

Stop sharing your location. Many forget that they granted someone else the ability to track them via "find my iPhone," "Life360," or various other apps.

When you get your oil changed, have the tech look under your car for tracking devices. Even though they are getting smaller, they often stand out because they were placed on your vehicle quickly.

Now a quick story about where the oil change tech made a big difference. A female was getting harassed to the point that she could not work. She told me that everywhere she went, day or night, there he was, Mr. Glasses (he wore goofy glasses). Day after day, he would show up, and when police were called, he would always manage to skip away just in time. One day, we had her leave her phone at home to rule out that he was tracking it. Since they had been a couple, this was a good strategy. She attempted to document him with a GoPro camera when he showed up again, but he simply covered his face and jogged out of the area. We then had her go to our favorite oil change place.

We had her tell the tech not to touch anything he found. After a few minutes, the tech showed her a picture of a tracker near the gas tank on his cell phone. We called the Sheriff's Department, and the Deputy documented and removed what he saw. Later, the Deputy called me to advise that the tracker was cellular, and they traced the sim card back to… Mr. Glasses. Since the state she was in considered it a crime (yes, not all do, and that gets complicated), an arrest warrant was issued for Mr. Glasses. This ultimately led to him losing his job and leaving the area.

Many companies sell remote surveillance items. Some look like construction cones, rocks, electrical boxes, and too many to list. We recommend taking pictures of your yard and road and knowing what's out there. If something shows up that is unusual, throw it away. Often, these devices are cellular, but some are WiFi, meaning the person is closer than you think. And yes, your cell phone can be a WiFi hotspot.

Beware of visitors. Sometimes the stalker has someone sympathetic to them and trying to help them. They can pose as a pizza delivery person, plumber, electrician, electric company, etc. We have seen them wear official shirts and carry equipment and clipboards for the ruse. What they don't have is the plumbing truck, delivery truck, etc. So take a look before you answer your door. Oh, and that official-looking shirt they are wearing might be from Goodwill or online.

MY WORST FEAR

From time to time, I get the question, what do you fear the most? Like most investigators, we fear connecting two people that should not be together. Can we find anyone? Yes, but that is not always good. When someone asks us to perform a locate, we perform searches to ensure they don't have a history of violence like assault and domestic-related items. If they say it's their lost sister, we look at our databases to confirm family members. It is a fear we have of sending a person to the address of someone who is hiding from them.

I will never forget a guy calling to tell me a long story about his sister, whom he was separated from when they were young. The parents could not afford the kids and had to give them both up for adoption. Something was just not right, although his story was very detailed and compelling. Liars often provide too much unnecessary detail. A family search did not reveal the sister, but she was young when they separated, per his story. I asked him to meet at a coffee place to discuss this. I wanted to see him in person to read him. Would he display signs of a liar, touching his nose in the middle of a story, voice inflections, facial expressions, and other body language signs? When we met, he was straightforward, had his story down, and showed no signs of being a liar. What he didn't know was that the family search had provided his parents and that he had two brothers. Did they not care about reuniting with their sister too? I let him talk, and he had an alarming amount of information about his sister. I searched for restraining orders, court documents, and more and saw nothing regarding him. I finally determined that something was just off. He even offered to pay me twice as much as I normally charge to get it done quickly. I then made him very angry. I pulled out a piece of paper with his parents' and siblings' phone numbers on it. Then I reached for my phone and started dialing his mom; he literally slapped my phone across the room and got very angry. The coffee manager made eye contact with me, searching if I needed help. I stood up, turned (yes, my gun was visible), picked up my phone, and left the coffee place. I did do the skip trace. I called the "sister" and found out she was a former employee of his that he had stalked for five years. She moved multiple times and was always certain he would find her. I spent an hour on the phone with her, giving advice. She told me that he would get access to her credit report and find out where she was. I helped her fix this. I take her call every time she calls to this day. I also learned from a call with his mother that he had a terrible childhood and abandonment issues growing up around her drug addiction and abusive husband.

One of the tactics if you're trying to confuse someone looking for you is simple. Since your credit cards all want to be paperless, agree to this. Now, let's say you have four credit cards. Log into each card and change your mailing address to one of their physical bank branch locations in another state. This works, too, for getting tickets at the residential rate to things like SXSW. Do this with each card, and guess what? Your credit report will reflect the new addresses. Pick different states and confuse your problem person even more.

Wait, this is a good time to tell you again to change your passwords!

I want you to have a plan and to run through the scenarios until it's muscle memory. A stalker shows up at the house; you don't panic. You KNOW what to do. You become a steward of documentation. You become your best asset. People get frozen, depressed, and suicidal. Yes, the person getting stalked can sometimes feel suicidal, helpless, and alone. Know that you are not alone. If you have non-supportive friends or family, talk to those in your life who understand. If you are a woman, a battered women's shelter can be an excellent haven. They will not talk. They will not give up their location and are prepared and experienced in your problem.

CHAPTER NINE

SOCIAL ENGINEERING

"Amateurs hack systems, professionals hack people."

- *Bruce Schneier*

Beware of Social Engineering. Hackers use it; one famous hacker even hacked major government sites and extracted information. Let me give you an example of a method we use when trying to confirm if someone indeed lives at an apartment complex. If we simply call and ask if Joe Jones lives there, they will tell us that they cannot give out that information. So how do we confirm? Other than looking for them walking in the parking lot to confirm their car is present, there is an easier way. Here is how the conversation goes:

Me – "Hi, I'm with Blah Blah flowers, and we've made two attempts to deliver to Joe Jones (our target). Can we just drop them off at the front office?"

The apartment Manager's response tells us what we want to know. "No, we don't have a resident by that name." or "Yes, you are welcome to drop them off here."

Without them knowing, they just confirmed what we wanted to know.

This plays into how hackers work too. The hacker has the last four digits of your Social Security Number and needs the first five. They see that you attended a college and then call the college. They are often transferred to a student earning credit in the admissions office to help you. Here is how that call goes:

Student Worker – "Hello, admissions."

Hacker – "Hi, we are considering a graduate from your school and want to verify that they actually graduated. Can you help me?"

Student Worker – "Yes, do you have their Social Security Number?"

Hacker – "I do, but I am at a coffee shop and don't want to say it out loud." Can I just give you their name and last four digits?"

Student Worker – "Yes, what are those details?"

Hacker – "Jane Doe and the last four are 1234 (remember this is all they have)." "By the way, you sound like a student. What are you studying (building rapport)?"

Student Worker – " I am studying Marketing, and yes, they attended here and received honors."

Hacker – "This place just cleared out, so can I verify the rest of the social security number? If I don't, my boss will complain."

Student Worker – "Sure, go ahead."

Hacker – "First, I have my degree in Marketing too, but you sound like you got better grades than me! (she laughs) I have the first three as 325."

Student Worker – "Oh, that's not what we have. We have 000."

Hacker – "That figures our hiring manager couldn't tie his own shoes (she laughs). I have the next two digits as 32 (remember he has no idea what these numbers are)."

Student Worker – "Wrong again. We show 86."

See what happened? She does not even know that she provided the missing links! The hackers love data breaches and Linkedin for your work history.

Now the hacker has the victim's full social security to open utilities (in another's name, cell phone accounts, etc.). Social Engineering works, and you need to be aware when you get a call asking you for details or only confirming information. You may be providing the missing piece of the puzzle.

Recently, we helped another investigator that was dealing with identity theft. He had to freeze his credit report and cards and send his mortgage company a cashier's check. What a pain! Originally, the only element the hacker did not have on him was his mother's maiden name. So, the hacker did some amazing Jedi moves that we have never seen! NOT! The hacker went to his Facebook, and under family members was his mom. And on her Facebook was her brother (same last name as the maiden name). It was that easy to get the missing piece from open and public social media. Don't make your friends public on Facebook. Living out loud has consequences.

CHAPTER TEN

CELEB LOVES HER PHONE

"The advance of technology is based on making it fit in so that you don't really even notice it, so it's part of everyday life."

- *Bill Gates*

Meet Mr. Act. He has had more than one stalker and has it all figured out. He once hired me to test all his strategies and was upset when his efforts failed. He had his property in a trust, cars in his business manager's name, and was good at keeping a low profile when in public. He blew a gasket when I showed him that his sports car's navigation system had a choice for "home," which took you right to his front door. One night, he took a new lady back to his place. She kept telling him she could help him redecorate and could see herself living there. They dated for a couple of months, and then he broke up with her. However, she did not like this and began calling and following him. She told him she could get to him anytime and anywhere. She showed up on his other dates and caused chaos. She also harassed anyone that she thought was getting close to him. To say the least, she was disrupting his life.

His house was not easy to find. It was up a steep hill, and you had to make a sharp turn at the driveway. So, when things like a baby stroller were left at the end of his driveway, he knew it had to be her. She would write him notes, and to this day, we are not sure how she got a note inside his locked car while it was parked on set in a gated parking garage at the studio. As time went on and as he continued to ignore her, things got worse. She went as far as to call his mother and say she was pregnant.

One evening, he was out for drinks with some friends, and when he returned to his car, it had a smashed windshield. A few nights later, someone threw a rock through his kitchen window. She, of course, denied it when contacted by the police. Once, after he boarded his dog while shooting out of state, she picked up the dog, posing as his assistant. Lucky for her, the dog kennel did not have working cameras in the lobby. She took the dog to his house, placing her in the yard with food and water. She was not cruel; she just wanted to show our client she had the upper hand. That was the last straw, and he asked me to assist. I found that although the dog kennel did not have a lobby camera, she probably had to sign for the dog, and sometimes under stress, people make mistakes. Her mistake?

Signing the release form using her real name! She did not want to, but it was the policy of the kennel to require a picture ID that matched a signature before releasing animals. This helped with the legal proceedings, as she denied all wrongdoings at every turn, court date, police visit, and interview. She was good, but she did not realize that your cell phone tells everything about you, like your location. She did not think about her phone activities, search history, map use, and even that she had <u>his</u> banking app to monitor all of his purchases. Through a lawsuit, we legally obtained her cell phone and showed that she was proven to be the person to pick up the dog, she was there the night the windshield was smashed, etc. Her cell phone was her worst enemy, telling all of her secrets.

She has moved on in recent months. After she served some time, she started stalking another guy. We fear for anyone that she is currently dating as she is determined. And how did she know where he was exactly all of those times? Because she had installed an app on his phone that allowed tracking, listening, and watching! This app was well hidden, and it was not until our cell phone expert examined his phone that it was discovered. If you think your cell phone is hacked, look for things like it lighting up for no reason, decreased battery life, and the data bar moving when you are not using it.

If you think your phone may be being monitored, look for apps like these:

nSpy

Cocospy

XNSPY

uMobix

Mobilespy

Hoverwatch

eyeZy

Spyera

Flexispy

pcTattletale

Minspy

SpyBubble

Spyier

Spyic

MobiStealth

iSpyoo

Do not ever jailbreak your iPhone or root your Android. It takes away your ability to protect yourself and your information.

IF YOU THINK YOUR CELLPHONE IS BEING WATCHED/HACKED

If you think your cellphone has spyware, do the following and know that it works for both Apple IOS and Android:

Just like you are making a call, dial *#21#, then hit call.

A list will pop up, and everything listed should be <u>disabled</u>. If one listed is ENABLED, call your cellphone provider and report as mentioned early.

Also, ensure you have stopped sharing your location via phone apps if you have previously granted it. What easier way to find you at all times than seeing you in real-time.

I write this next part to be included with the above as I have spoken with security teams about this many times, and it is a problem. Maybe this will help them see the problem.

After being called to a record label one day, I met with an artist, her tour manager, her security head for the tour, and her attorney. She had a serious stalker problem, and although she had beefed up security, she was terrified due to the death threats.

I asked a lot of questions and was frequently interrupted by the security person that they had that covered, had thought of that, and really did not know why anyone wanted me there. Me neither; why was I here? The head of the label spoke up and started praising me for my past work. I then had an idea. I told everyone in the room to take a good look at me. Now that everyone was certain what I looked like, I stated I would stick a red sticker on the artist within the next week, proving their security techniques would not work. The artist loved this, and the head of security laughed and told me I would likely be beaten up by his team. I then bet him a gift certificate to my favorite restaurant (I was confident) that I could do it within the stated time. Afterward, I departed and developed a plan.

Below is what I did, and I hope this helps security teams everywhere, as it can be a problem.

First, I looked at the tour schedule and venues. I wanted a venue with the most exits and a stage positioned in a certain way. It is important to know that the show time for the day of the show was 8:00PM. So, I showed up at 9:00AM at the venue. I wore all black and walked through the wide-open doors before security or the band arrived. It was load in, and only the local lighting crew they hired was present. I did not have any credentials whatsoever. And around 11:15 AM, the band, artist, and security showed up and started controlling the doors for sound check. Security was security theater at best. They walked around, looking bored and on their phones. By then, I was well-known to the workers at the venue, the lighting crew, and the merch people. When the tour manager walked by, I bent down, picked up a box, and carried it to another location. One of the lighting crew members pointed out I did not have a lanyard as required, and I said I had left it in the hotel. Their response? "Let me get you another one, as we must have them." They acquired one from the tour manager, and now I even looked completely official. As long as I avoided anyone I knew and was nice and dumb to everyone else, I was gold. After the sound check, the artist turned and was walking down the backstage steps when I slid out from under the stage and lightly attached the red sticker to her back as she walked past. Then it hit me: would it not be epic to put one on the head of security too? I walked around a bit, and then there he was, on his phone, yelling at someone. I walked up and patted him on the back (placing the red sticker) and said, "There are sandwiches on the bus." He only threw his hand up without turning.

I walked out of the venue but not before being thanked for helping lift a large crate. I called the head of the label and told him about the day and the security failures, and he was floored. He called the artist, who did not know the sticker was still on her back. She had gone straight to her bus and could not believe it. Needless to say, the head of security hates me to this day for making him look foolish. Honestly, that was my favorite part. He told the label that I must have worn a disguise or had someone else do it, as he had everyone looking for me. Good thing I wore a small body camera which proved I did not, as I started my day by talking in front of a mirror. They changed their tactics for the rest of the tour, and I got my gift card in addition to my fee. The label is still a client, and we, of course, identified the stalker: a crazed fan that lived with his mother, did not have a car or job and thought a song was about him. Crazy is forever!

CHAPTER ELEVEN

SOCIAL MEDIA

"Facebook was not originally created to be a company. It was built to accomplish a social mission – to make the world more open and connected."

- Mark Zuckerburg

DO NOT LIVE OUT LOUD

I love when people ask, "how did they know this about me?" When we coach celebrities, we teach them to not post in real-time. We have all heard people post that they are on vacation and get robbed. They don't know people can put their family tree together by watching their posts and who "likes" them.

Did you know that Venmo is actually a social media platform? When conducting investigations, we always look at Venmo. Who are they sending and receiving money from? How do those people connect? I was asked once if I could get the son's name in an insurance manner, and there it was on Venmo. Money transfers from dad for various expenses. Set your Venmo to private!

I need to point out that an obsessed person will spend hours on your social media. They will notice things you "liked," like thirty-two restaurants, sixteen bars, and only <u>one</u> local coffee place. If you have pictures of you drinking coffee, you just made a prime location to acquire you. Want to throw them off? Post about multiple coffee places. Try posting a picture holding a cup from one that is an hour away and continue to post about how amazing their coffee is. Or better yet, don't post anything about your love for coffee or where you get it.

"Likes" and "check-ins" are a giveaway, an open door to your activities. If you have checked into a local church, you probably go there. If you recommend a hair salon, the same. Did you know that if I call a hair salon and say I want to buy my wife a $250.00 gift card but I don't know when her next appointment is, they will most likely tell me? Again, think like a stalker and stop them.

We have said early to be cautious of links in emails and texts. But what about sending things out? Facebook is good about not providing the geo-locations of posted pictures. However, if someone can get you to send them a picture directly, they have the location, time, and date the picture was taken. We did a case where the person was selling a car on craigslist and being stalked. In the ad, they said they would meet the buyer at the local police station for a safe exchange. The stalker posed as a buyer and asked them to email additional pictures. Then they used the geolocation of the photos to get the location of their secret residence. You must always be alerted that photos can tell a lot about you. A picture is worth a thousand words and can tell a thousand secrets too.

FAKE ACCOUNTS

You are getting harassed and concerned about adding anyone to your social media. Every time you get a request, you freeze and are concerned you may let the problem back into your life. Since stalkers like to create fake accounts, here are some ways to spot them:

- Following several accounts but has no followers
- Few, if any, posts
- Only reposts others' content
- Profile picture used on other accounts
- Liking really old posts of yours
- No written content

These are just a few, and there are many more. Regarding the profile picture used on other accounts, download their photo and head to sites like TinEye.com and Google images. Use their search-by-image tool to see if those profile pictures appear on additional profiles. Once confirmed that the account is fake, block it.

YOU KNOW TO LIE – DOES YOUR FAMILY?

I had a case where a lady was claiming total disability. First, she moved to a new residence and used a UPS box. To observe her activities, we needed to know where she was. We started monitoring her social media and her family members' open and public social media. One day, her daughter posted a picture of our claimant standing on the front porch of their new residence. In the background were the four digits of the address. Since she had a history of renting homes, we went to work looking for rentals in the area with those numbers. A few minutes later, we pulled up the correct address with the same porch, windows, and front door. We obtained what we needed, but the icing on the cake was when her daughter posted a video of her on Instagram at an axe-throwing business. The post was up for 17 minutes before being deleted. Too late; we already had it and were sending it to the insurance company!

There is so much more to social media, so I intend to write another book just on that subject.

Additionally, we always tell clients that their parents may know to tell a lie about them, but do their grandparents?

When asked to find a man involved in a hit-and-run accident with no insurance that caused permanent disability to a father of four, we pulled out all the stops. When we called the driver's employer, he had quit. When we contacted family and friends, we were told he had moved to Mexico. His social media also stated that he was residing in Mexico, but we did not believe it. We doubted he had a passport or the means to get there. One afternoon, I called his grandmother and said I was an old friend that owed him money, and since he spoke so highly of her, she was who I remembered as a relative. She told me that she had just seen him (not in Mexico) and that he was working at a nearby Fire Station on Main Street. Grandma was not told to lie! I thanked her and asked her to keep the surprise to herself. We then headed to the Fire Station. He did not work there, and after showing his picture to the captain, he laughed and showed it to another firefighter. "Isn't that the guy a Firehouse Subs down the street?" They both agreed, and we walked down to the restaurant. And there he was, waiting on a customer in the United States. We served him and filmed it, but we did not stop there. Since he had an outstanding warrant for unpaid child support and a DUI, we waited until after his shift and followed him to his sister's house, where he was living. A short time later, he was arrested, and it was proven that his mother had insurance on the car he was driving at the time of the accident. When people ask other's to lie, they often only include the people in their immediate circle!

CHAPTER TWELVE

IS TECH GOOD

"The people who are crazy enough to think they can change the world are the ones who do."

- *Steve Jobs*

First, I love Apple and most things Apple. I have their stock and many products. My love for Apple products was born after having lunch with my attorney, and she showed me many features. Yes, that was a while ago. I have an Apple watch, which I use to tell the time, like most people. And like most people, we only use it to tell the time. Since murder cases have been proven using the Apple watch (the murderer's pulse rate rose at the time of someone's murder), it tells on you more than you might expect. I used mine for oxygen levels, heart rate, and some apps but lost interest overall. The fact that it knew my sleep patterns, or lack of them, interested me.

As mentioned earlier, your cell phone tells so much about you that it is truly scary. Your information is likely backed up in a cloud, and you have probably forgotten about all the apps you have granted permission. Your phone knows everything about you and can't wait to tell everyone that will listen.

Apple AirTags are a great invention. They can track your luggage or lost keys and use other iPhones to pinpoint what you are tracking. The problem is that stalkers started using them as car trackers, personal trackers, and more. Apple addressed this, and the AirTag will chirp if it detects that another device is moving to all the same locations and alert their phone. They are small, and if a stalker accidentally left one in your car or, say, a key ring with useless keys and the sound was muffled, who would know? If confronted by police, the stalker could say, "I have been looking everywhere for those keys and forgot they had an AirTag on them." Yeah sure. But that kind of thing will get dismissed after causing you headaches. Luckily, since AirTags are connected to the owner's iTunes account, they can be traced back to the account associated with it if the owner is unknown.

Let me ask you this, would you openly tell a stranger where you bank? Probably not. We will sometimes be asked to do asset checks for law firms to assess the person's net worth. If the firm gets a judgment, they often look for bank accounts and employers to garnish. So, what's an easy way to get their bank? Walk up and ask them a question requiring them to pull out their smartphone. Like, "Do you have the number of the person in charge of your homeowner's association?" Often, right there on the home screen is a banking app for their bank. Just be observant, right? Only stalkers think this way, too; they study your phone to determine a lot of things about you. Would you randomly use the Planet Fitness app if you did not work out there? Probably not. If you have the Starbucks app, you likely go there for coffee. How about the American Airlines app? I am guessing that is your airline of choice. Get a screen protector that allows only direct viewing to see what is on your phone. It is a good investment and will protect you from prying eyes.

When I had some family members head overseas for a vacation, I had them carry three ways to track them. First, their phones. Second, AirTags. And third, a satellite device. The AirTags were worn on each person, and I purchased clothing pins on Amazon to hold the trackers. This made everyone feel better and safer. But who else thinks like this?

I had a case where our client broke up with a person. The girl did not accept this and demanded that he see her. This went on for almost a year. At a meet-and-greet, he noticed a female in line walking a certain way. It was her; she was there to rekindle their love and patch things up. Instead, he had security escort her out, pushing her over the top. She started sending him notes and texts and showing up at his favorite stores and gym. He would say that if he went to a restaurant, she would be there within minutes. She was somehow tracking him. We started eliminating items when he left his house and ultimately determined it was his vehicle. If his vehicle traveled there, it was like she was in it too. For a test, I drove the vehicle one evening to a Walmart parking lot. We sat until she drove past, trying to look inside. We then drove it to a shop that would likely block all signals.

Upon inspecting the vehicle, a device was plugged into the OBD2 port under the dash. It honestly looked like it should be there. This is the port where auto mechanics plug in to see why you have a check engine light. We did not remove it. We simply had him get a restraining order and then wait at the police station for her to arrive. She did and had to answer for the tracker. Know your vehicle and know if something has been added or is missing.

DO YOU WORK HERE?

A client was happy to report that after moving across country, they no longer dealt with the harassment of a previous girlfriend. His new job was on the west coast, and he had heard she had finally married. After five years, he was moving up as an executive at his tech company and had just bought a new Porsche. Life was good.

When he posted that he had broken up with his current girlfriend and was heading to the mountains to clear his head, he posted a picture of him eating at his favorite taco bar at the beach. He used #MyFavoriteTacos. He left and enjoyed his weekend.

When he returned, he worked for a few weeks and decided to return to his favorite taco place. Behind the counter was a familiar face. She acted like this was a chance meeting, a sign from God. "What are the odds that I would move out here after my divorce and get a job at a place you would visit?" she said. Only, it was completely by design. Yes, she was divorced, and later when we spoke with her ex-husband, we knew she was truly violent. When our client asked the manager about hiring her, he responded that they needed people, and she was nice and had experience. And so, it all started over again, only this time, it was worse. When rejected, she tried to get him fired from his job. She also claimed that he had hit her. After providing pictures of her face with a bruise, she filed charges against him. She would also call the police and say that he was leaving her apartment after threatening her. She became the victim, and it almost got him fired. He called and asked for advice.

The local police department would not believe me when I told them she was putting all this on. They told me he was an abusive alcoholic (he did not drink), and if they caught him driving, they would pull him over and arrest him. We had an uphill battle to prove his innocence since everyone believed she was the victim. I had him install a call recording app on his phone, and he finally answered when she called. I coached him on what to say, and when he asked what he could do to make it stop, she said, "Marry me." The gal who was so scared that she ran into a police department like she had been chased inside just asked him to get married to her. He asked about her facial bruises, and she laughed that it was make-up. He asked why she was trying to get him fired, and she said, "So we can both move home to be together."

Her background check showed multiple domestic violence charges, stalking, assault, and two DUIs. I guess the police did not have time to run her records as we did. To add to the battle, she was very pretty and presented as an intelligent, nice, caring person.

In the end, we recorded multiple calls with her admitting to moving there to be with him and that she tried to get him fired to ruin his life so she could help him heal. She thought, "If his life is not with me, he does not deserve to have a good one." His company was understanding after we presented the recordings to them. The police, however, still did not want to listen and ignored our presentation. He ultimately got the court to listen, and it was finally over. After the dust settled, we made it look like he had moved away to Canada. Since she had no reason to stay, she left the area.

How did this start up again? By him accepting friend requests from pretty girls, real or not. That is how she got back in, with a fake profile and some seductive pictures. Be careful who you are friending as it might just reopen a past door you wanted to stay closed.

ALL HE WANTED WAS TO HEAR "I LOVE YOU"

Let me introduce Ms. Elly. She was a past beauty queen and spokesperson for a nonprofit. She was a leader in her church and would walk a mile to give you a bottle of water if you were thirsty. She was as nice as anyone you have ever met and was always polite. One afternoon, she was coaching a young girl on how she wore Vaseline on her teeth at parades to keep smiling. A man walked in, and they made eye contact for a brief moment.

To her, it was just another person walking past an auditorium. To him, it was love at first sight, and he thought it was mutual.

After weeks of her being nice and rejecting his invitations for dates, he showed up at her apartment at 3:15AM and knocked on the door until she answered. She was again very nice as he told her about a movie he had just seen that reminded him of her. He stood at the door until she nicely asked him to leave. Instead of leaving, he walked past her into her apartment and turned on the TV. He said the movie was on a streaming service and that they should sit and watch it together. She was scared and did not know what to do. She lived alone and only really knew a friend in the next building. Should she call the police? Would that ruin his life? She faked that she had to use the restroom, and he seemed unbothered. She locked the door and called her friend when she got into her bedroom. The friend and her boyfriend came over and made the man leave, threatening to call the police. He was clearly upset and confused.

A few days later, she was getting gas, and he walked up to her and said, "I don't know why you won't just talk to me!" She was shaken and asked him to leave. He started talking about how their kids would look and where they could live. A police officer pulled into a nearby gas pump bay, and she immediately walked over to him. She told the officer that the man would not leave her alone. The officer asked him for ID, and the man turned, ran to his car, and departed the area.

The officer told her there was not much he could do. She left the gas station and went to her apartment. The next morning, she walked out to see a rose, a bottle of wine, and a note apologizing for his behavior. The note said, "How am I ever going to hear I love you if you won't talk to me." She knew this was beyond infatuation and called her father. Her dad and I met at a football game a couple of years earlier. When he told me how things were progressing, we asked if she knew his name? She did not. How did he know where she lived? He did not know.

We visited the apartment and interviewed the girl. She said he would just show up and try to get through her door. I spoke with the apartment security, but they had no camera footage. We decided to wait for him at her apartment. It did not take long until his Chevy Malibu entered the parking lot. He bounced out of the car like he was late for dinner and went straight to her door. I followed and acted like I was her neighbor. After asking who he was, he replied that all I needed to know was to stay away from his fiancée! What? I walked down the stairs, obtained his license plate, and went to work. The vehicle came back to an 86-year-old man across town. When the man came down after thinking she wasn't home, I asked if he could help me. I played nice and dumb. I was uninterested in his girl as I was married and needed to use his phone as mine was dead. He snapped that he did not have a phone as the government listens to everything people talk about. I smiled, told him I needed a job, and asked if his place of employment was hiring. He stated he was on disability and did not have to work. He then called me a name and drove away.

I had one of my associates follow him, and after 20 minutes of driving, he pulled into a self-service car wash, where he sat for more than an hour. I advised discontinuing the pursuit.

Later that night, I drove past the residence where the plate led us to. Surprisingly, the car was not present.

The next morning, I drove by again, and an older man was standing outside the residence, working on his flowers. I stopped and started a conversation. Ultimately, I learned that the man was his nephew and lived in an old house down the street. He let him use the car as the older man could no longer drive, and the nephew took him to his doctor's appointments. I obtained his first name and went down to the rough, almost abandoned-looking house where he lived. It was noted that the Chevy Malibu was present and tucked in tight near the house, making it invisible from the public road. A neighbor was out, so I struck up a conversation. Once again, I played nice and dumb and learned who the landlord was (the home was in the name of an Oregon Company) and called him. After a lengthy conversation and some pretexting, I learned the man's last name and that he liked to hang out at a market (the landlord advised that rent was paid with prepaid cards from a specific market). Later, I confirmed that the market was next to the auditorium where he first met our girl.

I went to the market and spoke with the people hanging out there. They knew the man well as he had spent a lot of time there. They also said that he was to be engaged and planned on having kids shortly after getting married. He would even point out the girl sometime from a distance as she left the coaching sessions at the auditorium. I left quickly after seeing the Chevy Malibu approaching the market.

I called the girl's father, and we agreed that the traditional route would not resonate with this guy. We then set up a plan. Phase one: she had to move. Phase two: she would no longer coach at the auditorium. Finally, phase three: we would tell him that she moved to Europe. All went well, and yes, he visited the apartments many times after she left. We instructed the apartments and the neighbors to say she had moved away to France. She started coaching her students remotely and ensured everyone knew not to mention she was still in town. Then it went south. One of the girls went to the market with her mom and talked about an upcoming beauty pageant, adding that her coach would be there to cheer for her.

When it was time for the pageant, our man was there. Our girl immediately saw him and ran to her car. Worried, she called us, and we quickly formulated a backup plan, and I called an actor friend. He did not understand when I requested that he wear a dark suit. I changed my appearance and escorted the girl into the pageant, and when it was over, we walked her out. The man immediately approached us and started asking her where she had been and why she had lied. Since we knew everything about the man, we took a risk. I told him she was engaged and that her man worked for the Federal Government. As my actor friend walked up, he played along. We knew everything about him, where he lived, his uncle, the car, his disability checks, and his landlord, and we were watching him. The man was speechless. He apologized to the girl and said, "I just wanted to hear you say I love you." He looked at her with disgust and disappointment. He has not been a problem since. This was only attempted after multiple interviews with neighbors to properly profile him. This is not recommended and knowing that she was willing to relocate at any time is important.

Being stalked is traumatic. If you know someone being stalked, believe and support them. Often, the stalked feel alone and that no one believes them.

CHAPTER THIRTEEN

PIC AND CALLS

"It's ironic that this amazing invention of the Internet has made information gathering easier available than ever, but that this platform also helps spread misinformation."

- *Will.i.am*

We had a case where we tried everything to make a guy stop contacting a receptionist at a music publishing company. Because she answered the phone for her job, he frequently used Google Numbers and called from other places to talk to her. He would disguise his voice, tell her she looked nice today, and describe what she was wearing. He loved to hear her voice.

Her car was in the shop one day, and she took an Uber to work. When he called using a spoof card (a card that allows you to put whatever you want on someone's caller ID), he used her sister's cell phone as the display number. When she answered, he asked if the repair shop she chose was the best place to take her car for its starting issues. He then proceeded to ask if she gave the Uber driver 5 stars. He would not stop.

Her boyfriend at the time started getting harassed too. He was a bartender and was ultimately fired from his job after the bar got a tip that he was stealing money and giving free drinks. This was not true. At his next job, the same tips came in, and as a result, he ended the relationship with her because he said he could not take the harassment.

Now she was alone, depressed, and feared everywhere she went. The owner of the publishing company had me sit down with her. He even paid our retainer to get her help. After the interview, we went to work. The stalker was much older than her and had met her at a music event she was attending for the publishing company's songwriters. This was not an invitation event; he was just hanging out in the bar when she caught his eye. He offered to buy her a drink, and she refused, stating she had a boyfriend. He kept talking to her and saying things like "You need a man that treats you right" and various sexual comments relating to her appearance. The bouncer finally had to ask him to leave, and as he departed, he told her, "I'll see you real soon." When we later determined his employment, we confirmed that he was working remotely from home as an IT person. He lived alone in a normal neighborhood and had no family.

She had done all the right things: filed all the correct paperwork, and the police had an open file regarding her case. He, however, was not afraid of anything, had a good attorney, and never seemed to get into trouble due to the harassment. All the resources in place to help her seemed to fail because he had a real job and was smart. When asked, "Why were you outside of her apartment on said date?" he would always have an answer like, "I am considering moving there. I thought this was a free country, and I could go anywhere!"

We had to think outside the box. He was smart and determined. Since he had no prior record, arrests, and stalking-related charges, he seemed to glide through the system. I think to this day, he somehow enjoyed the legal ride and liked having power over her. We started recording every call at the publishing company, noting every email and every time he showed up around her. He monitored her social media, and although he was blocked and her profile was private, he always managed to know what she was doing.

I then called a friend of mine that was a local police officer. I asked if I could hire him to do a type of "special duty" when he was off. I explained the situation, and he agreed. We had her post a picture of him (my friend) in plain clothes on her locked-down Instagram with the caption, "I have never been happier." Our stalker mentioned the post on his next call to her. We conducted security and made sure she was not followed one day and without her phone. Then we literally had the officer, and her do a photo shoot for a few hours. They changed clothes and locations frequently, and it was good to see her laugh again.

She posted a picture of her sitting in her car with the police department in the fuzzy distance. Her caption said, "Lunch today" and "It's always a good day with the man of your dreams." This made the stalker very curious.

We even had the officer stop by her office on a few occasions on his days off for lunch. At lunch, they would try to sit outside or near a window. Luckily, they were always laughing and smiling because of the progress they were making.

All of the next series of daily posts on her locked-down Instagram was of him in uniform. She was excited to date a police officer and made it public. The calls stopped. The harassment stopped. For weeks, her posts would be about being in love with this police officer, and life returned to normal. When the officer's name was discovered by the stalker, it only made it more convincing. The harassment moved to strictly social media after we noted that the IT pro had remote access to her computer and camera. There is a reason that Steve Jobs placed tape over his laptop camera!

It was painstaking, but we had her delete all social media (after we documented everything), wait two months, start with new accounts, and be very selective about followers. She changed all passwords, and we had experts review her laptop and cell phone to confirm there was no malware. Because of her diligent efforts and willingness to play along, the stalking stopped. She is now stalker free and living a happy, normal life with her new man, a songwriter. Sometimes the right pictures and be very valuable.

SHOULD YOU DELETE SOCIAL MEDIA?

Not necessarily, as it is a source of evidence.

TIPS

- Screenshot social media harassment and upload it to a shared cloud service like dropbox and share with trusted friends or family

- Report harassment to the social media platform

- Don't post personal information

- Don't "like" your actual favorite bars, restaurants, and coffee locations

- Don't identify family members

- Don't list your employer

- Document all accounts that are harassing, as it may be the same person

- Don't post in real-time

- Don't communicate with stalkers

Are you aware that you can see someone else's location on Snapchat? Think like a stalker, and don't share. Many YouTube videos explain how to set your social media to private. Don't make it easy to ever see where you are.

We assisted in a case where we interviewed the client and then worked to lock down all her social media. The stalker was a boyfriend with whom she had gone on less than ten dates. He told her on their first date that she reminded him of his mother a lot. He told her on a subsequent date that he hated his mother and that she was now deceased. When she asked how his mother passed, he said he disliked talking about it but was happier now.

Late one night, she decided to google the death of his mother and learned that she had fallen from a barn loft. The report stated that her son had not reported it for nearly a week and had already had her cremated by the time he reported it. This and many other reasons, such as him constantly wanting to know where she was and who she was with, led her to end the relationship. She was nice when she broke up with him, and he did not get the message. He showed up at her work, her weekly bible study, and a yoga class that started at 5:30AM. We worked hard to ensure no locations were being shared anywhere and had her change her church and yoga location and work remotely. We even worked with her daughter to lock down her own social media. But kids will be kids.

One day, the client received a message from her friend telling her that her daughter's Snapchat was showing a location, a rural property outside of town. Yes, it was the hidden location residence we had worked so hard to hide. This little fault resulted in headaches. It would be best to communicate the importance of your safety with your children. The client has since moved to another state, and the stalker has moved on to another girlfriend he met, you guessed it, on a dating app. We sent the new girlfriend a message hoping to save her from the same problems that the client dealt with. Her response? She wrote back, saying she would be the difference in his life. She understood him and would work through any problems that they had.

CHAPTER FOURTEEN

DATING

"A woman knows by intuition, or instinct, what is best for herself."

- *Marilyn Monroe*

Walk Prepared / Dating & Dating Apps

I recently watched on social media how some New York mobsters who would "shake down" commercial property owners never bothered Donald Trump. This is not a political context but a security one. They did not bother Trump because he hired ex-FBI agents as his security detail before becoming president. They did not want to deal with taking on an organization as they were looking for easier targets.

This is in line with what we tell our celebrity clients. Posting pictures with a security detail is a deterrent, only we don't have them post with their actual security detail. A celebrity stalker will want an easier target than one with four ex-Navy Seals walking with them. If a stalker plans to head to a rural residence and fears being met with strong opposition, they may change their mind. The thought of sneaking up to a dark window and not seeing the well-trained marksman walking up silently behind them is a good fear.

Even if the celebrity has no security detail, we recommend showing posts with fake detail. This simple show of force makes a would-be problem place their focus somewhere else.

In the case of Ms. D, this worked brilliantly. One summer night, Ms. D was sitting out by her pool when she heard a noise on the other side of her fence. When she went to investigate, she saw a man limping, stating that he had fallen in the nearby woods and was hurt. Her intuition was saying he was lying. She had just had lunch with us, discussing not ignoring what your subconscious is trying to warn you about. She offered to call help for him, but he instead wanted to just come into the pool area and rest. He said he had sent for an Uber, and since they were located outside of town, it would take approximately 40 minutes. She paused and did not go against her intuition. Instead, she started calling for "Robert and James" to investigate and help this guy. She also picked up her phone and called the police immediately. When he asked who Robert and James were, she said they were part of her security detail and would be there momentarily. The man looked startled and started looking all around. Once the police answered, she did not say she was in danger. Instead, she told them her security team needed assistance with a hurt man on her property. The man, the one with the hurt leg, turned and ran up into the woods. The fact that she was alert and calm and told him she had security potentially saved her life. When the police arrived, she described the man who was dressed too nicely to be out hiking at night and did not have ripped pants or dirt on him. The police caught up with him a couple of miles away, where he had parked his car. In his car were pictures of her and several guns.

As Wikipedia defines, Security Theater is "The practice of taking security measures that are considered to provide the feeling of improved security while doing little or nothing to achieve it." I used this example because I agree.

Security Theater is like when you go to the airport and have to take your shoes off because one guy that boarded a plane was a problem. It is a show of force with no real protection. And it works! A single female that places a large pair of men's muddy work boots outside her door or turns when she leaves her apartment and yells inside the empty room, "I love you, and I will see you later or are you still going to the gym?" is a good practice. Like a client that faked an argument once while she was home alone, and her problem person was outside. She yelled at her imaginary boyfriend, saying, "Another assault will surely send you back to prison." Placing a "My man is a proud marine" or "Guns don't kill people, I do" on your vehicle may be more effective than you realize.

We also have a client who only takes pictures for social media with the biggest bouncers they can find when they are out at the Broadway bars. It has become a running joke that she should have an award for the largest bouncer in Nashville.

Women drive cars, and men drive trucks. Not true? Imagine you are a stalker that follows a girl out of a bar, and she gets into a lifted camo covered Chevy truck. Would you assume it is her vehicle or her redneck boyfriend's truck? Changing the perception of how people see you can grant some safety.

I often see women walking home from bars talking on a cell phone for safety. What I, and perhaps a stalker, see is a woman with a hand that is not free to protect herself and a person too far away to help her. If she is grabbed and the phone is tossed, what leads other than perhaps a video from a business or residence showing her being carted away would exist? It is better to have wireless air buds while walking and talking with a real or imaginary person, alert and ready to fight, if necessary. Carrying a weapon on a key change you are prepared to use is wise. I'm not a huge fan of mace or pepper spray, as people often spray it in the wrong direction or can't get it to spray at all. Or worse yet, spray themselves. Taking a self-defense class is highly recommended. Remember that a guy hit in the nose, eyes, throat, and private area will feel it with your hand and regret it if you're carrying something harder than your hand. Be prepared to run. If you have on high heels, take them off and throw them at him. It's better to buy a new pair of shoes and be able to run away yelling for assistance. Remember that when you are yelling, people pay attention to "fire" more than "help." People don't want to get involved with the drama of someone yelling "help" but will pay attention when you yell "fire!"

Always be ready and have your hands free. Watch out for overly friendly, helpful people who need a woman that's alone for assistance. And beware of people that don't take no for an answer. Remember Ted Bundy asking for help with a fake sling on his arm or the nut in the movie *Silence of the Lambs* asking for help loading a couch into his van? There are many unsolved murders and missing people in the files of police departments across America. Do not be a statistic; be like a predator. Fight back always.

Here is a scenario: a guy pulls up in a car, holds up a gun, and tells you to get into the car. What do you do? I can tell you that your odds of survival drop significantly if you enter the car. The car is likely headed somewhere isolated. Make your fight in the present. Right there and right then. And run in the vehicle's blind spot away from the car while yelling. He will likely speed away. While you are standing on a street, there are more cameras and witnesses than there will be at his intended destination. Be the hero of your story, not the victim.

Lately, there seem to be more abductions via a car pulling up and a female entering it because they thought it was their ride-share ride. First, how did they profile you? Were you standing in a corner, looking at your phone at every car that drove nearby? Look at your app and confirm what the driver is driving. Google a bigger picture of the vehicle if you are unsure what a Ford Explorer looks like. And do not get into the vehicle unless you confirm the driver's name and they confirm yours. <u>Let them do the talking</u>. Do not say, "Are you Ralph?" Instead, ask for their name first. Then ask them for your name. Ask which ride-share company they are with, a question rarely asked. Take a picture of their license plate, then the driver, and send it to a friend. If they are legit, they probably won't care. If they are not, they will likely speed away.

Being drunk is a fun time for many. Being drunk and alone on the street is not recommended. I see drunk women walking from the bars on Broadway in Nashville every night of the week. They are easy to spot as they stumble, walk recklessly, or close their eyes very slowly as they try to focus. They usually have a cell phone occupying one hand and a purse occupying the other. Do not advertise that you are an easy victim; don't walk alone if you have been drinking. Nashville is growing so fast that the police struggle to keep up. After your attack, you often just fill out paperwork regarding your incident. "What color was the man's shirt?" "I don't remember as I was drunk" is not a good combination if you seek justice.

If I sound like a preachy father, good. Your safety is important, and the world is dangerous enough without you making it easy. Be aware and be prepared.

DATING APPS

If you are on a dating app, it is ok to google and background your potential date. We get many requests for this, and I recommend it. You would not likely get into a stranger's car, but you'll meet at a bar on the edge of town. On the app, you are looking at a picture that you hope is the actual person (yes, they can be faked) and setting a time and a place where you will be. Ask questions before you meet.

Here are some good questions:

DATING APP QUESTIONS

- Where do you work? (call and confirm or have them email you from their work email. Example: Bob@HisIncredibleFunEmployer.com)

- Review their social media (sometimes an ex's post can save you a lot of time)

- Ask for their cell phone (don't call it and use your second number to text)

- Ask about their relationship with their mom and dad (abusers often have a bad relationship)

- Ask which area of town they reside in (say you live in a large subdivision)

- Run a basic search for their name with search terms like arrest and felony

- Ask about their longest relationship (if all their relationships are short, there is likely a reason)

- Ask about their ex, as this will reveal how they will talk/post about you later

- Search the local county website for civil suits and criminal records

- Ask what they will be wearing for the date to identify them

- How many matches have they had on this app?

- What other dating apps are you on? (Tinder is a good indication they may just want to hook up and not be seeking a long-term relationship)

- Where else have they lived? (check the states and areas they mention)

- Check LinkedIn from a fake profile you create to see if their employment matches what they tell you

- Ask if they've been married (reading a divorce decree can reveal a lot)

- Ask if they have a criminal record (if they say no and you find one, beware)

- A simple question like, "What color are your eyes?" may be answered before they remember that their fake profile image had a different color

- Ask for their social media handles (people often use the same handle as the profiles they did not want you to know about)

If they are disturbed by the above questions, this may have saved you a lot of time and potential headaches later. Yes, it may look excessive, but you can ask the same questions on the date to see if you get the same answers. This is a great way to identify a liar and thus save you from being lied to in the future.

If YOU are asked where you work, live, work out, party, etc., say things like, "I work in finance" instead of "I work at ABC Bank on Main Street." "I live in walking distance of my work," when you actually don't. If your match works out long-term, you can tell them later that this was for your protection as there are a lot of problem people out there. They will understand and likely be proud of you for being safety-minded.

In this hook-up society, I am frequently amazed that people will invite someone they just met back to their residence, have them spend the night, and leave them alone when they go to work the next morning. Yes, we have dealt with some problems in the aftermath of this decision, including identity theft, the copying of keys, stolen money, stolen items, and, of course, a stalker. You might think of it as just sex and a night well live, whereas the other person may think it is their lifelong love that they cannot relinquish.

Imagine you have a date scheduled for Friday night, and your background search provides that your match has a past stalking charge with a knife. Would you keep the date? Probably not; however, many women are going on a date tonight, counting on blind luck to keep them safe!

Here is a quick example of a dating app problem. Our client had a match, a perfect match. If they liked broccoli covered in champagne and grape jelly, so did their match. If they wanted to scale a building dressed like a dinosaur, so did this other profile. It was a match made in heaven, but there was a problem. When I got the call to see if the person on the other side of the dating app match was using their real name, I went to work. First, their profile picture was a picture of a model in Brazil (thank you, TinEye.com), and their interests were made to match our client's. We had her ask for their cell number, and they provided a VOIP (Voice Over Internet Protocol) number, which is very hard to trace! We had her ask a series of questions like the list above, and they answered spot on. They were well rehearsed. There were no leads, and the date was fast approaching.

We opted for another approach because she absolutely demanded to meet this guy. We would go to the date location with her, see if the guy was real, and then text her to enter the bar. This would allow us to send her a picture prior to her entering a confined space. The chosen location by him was a bar on the county line. The date night came, and she sat in our surveillance vehicle with dark windows, and we entered the bar 45 minutes early. We noted that this was a small bar with a dark parking lot. While she sat in our surveillance vehicle, guess who actually showed up? Her ex! He walked around the parking lot looking at the vehicles. This was a set-up to catch her away from her unknown residential location. He had constructed a dating profile of her exact likes to make the match easy. After filming him, we simply walked out of the bar and drove the surveillance vehicle away. It was noted that his vehicle was parked in a dark alley behind the bar's back door. He did not see her and was immediately on the app a short time later asking where she was? She said she had become sick and was heading to urgent care. When he asked which urgent care, she stopped responding. Why this location of a bar? We think he likely believed that the restraining order was limited to the county.

The police were called but arrived long after he had left. The security cameras at the bar did not have any positions outside, which I am sure he was aware of.

She deleted her profile and is still safe. He, on the other hand, is in more trouble as we filmed his presence at the bar and spoke to law enforcement regarding his fake dating ploy. We went as far as having the bartender sign an affidavit that no people were known to him, to be meeting at the bar from a match on a dating app that night. He denied it; however, his chances of showing up at the same bar exactly the same time she did via a dating match were not believed.

One more, for good measure. People meet in bars, churches, coffee places, work, and many more locations. Meeting someone in person allows you to observe their body language and make a determination if you want to continue. Meeting someone on a dating app can run risks. I am a fan of "It's Just Lunch," the dating connection that you meet simply for lunch. Tell your match that you Ubered there if you walked and that you walked if you drove there. No one needs to get your full picture on the first date.

Be aware of everything you tell a date about yourself. It may sound crazy, but taking notes after a date will help you later if they mention something you did not tell them and claim you did. Imagine you are alarmed by your date telling you what high school you attended and then saying, "You told me that after I told you what high school I went to. Remember?" A quick look at your notes would show they may be too invested in you.

If you're dating, have fun but be safe! I hate to be the one to tell you this but take the advice of George Costanza. Remember the Seinfeld episode where he decided to do the opposite of what he would normally do? Sometimes people are attracted to the wrong type of person due to past experience. They say women marry a man like their dad. If your father was abusive, you might want to think like George and change where and how you meet people and the type of person you really want to be with. If you think you can change a man, you're wrong. Ask the oldest and longest married couple you know if the things that drive them crazy about the other person were revealed early in their relationship. The answer will be yes, but they likely ignored it!

CHAPTER FIFTEEN

D.E.A.T.H

"You may have read that I went to M.I.T. In 1982 I filled out a Who's Who survey with joking responses, and they never bothered to check the facts."

- *Chevy Chase*

Before writing this book, I had lunch with a friend who heads a task force. He advised me to have an acronym to express an idea that would be easy to remember. I thought for a moment and then blurted out what came to mind first. Here it is:

D.E.A.T.H.

D.E.A.T.H. should be taken seriously. It is final. First, let me explain. Fear is a powerful tool when it comes to stalking. A stalker can use fear to control when a victim is willing to leave their home. They can make the victim lose their job, friends, family, and self-worth. They can make other people think the victim is acting crazy or being dramatic. Hitler used fear to control a country, and in the words of the late comedian Norm MacDonald, "Who did Germany go to war with?" "THE WORLD!"

Fear is a motivator. It motivates us not to walk down a dark alley, walk on the ledge of a 50-story building, and not pick up spiders and snakes. If a stalker was raised in fear by an abusive father or mother, they are more likely to use fear as a method of persuasion. If you were slapped every time you asked for a glass of water, you would likely stop asking.

I have seen stalkers leave scary items on victims' porches and notes, threatening to kill them if they were outside after 8:00PM. If you were told you would be killed for coming outside after 8:00PM, you would call the police. How many evenings after 8:00PM do you think the police would sit at your house for protection? The stalker knows this and works to instill fear at every chance they can. Fear is control. I'm often told the fear of not knowing what will happen next is the worst.

So, what does a stalker want?

Some want to:

- Continue a relationship

THINK LIKE A STALKER AND STOP THEM

- Believe they are in a relationship with you
- Want to ruin your life
- Want to get any attention they can
- Feel like they have been mistreated
- Control someone
- Have a distorted view of your relationship
- Believe that persistence will win you over
- Resolve a dispute
- Want you to notice them
- Be a menace
- Hurt you
- Think of you as their possession
- Believe you will change your mind

Often, the stalker is the victim in their own story and can be getting the revenge they so desperately want. These days of cyberstalking allow someone to stalk from anywhere in the world. You not sleeping for a week brings them joy and the feeling of accomplishment.

So, what does D.E.A.T.H. stand for?

First, you must tell someone you have a problem and seek assistance. Being isolated and quiet is a bad combination. Since you'll likely have to do the data collection yourself to present to the police and the court, you will need to *Document* everything. Every call, email, text, post, message, video clip, and location visit.

D – Document

E – Every

A – Attempt

T – To

H – Harass

Death is a strong word. Death should be taken seriously. D.E.A.T.H. could help you remember to use our provided form.

For years, I have said that if a person is served with a restraining order, they should have to wear a device that alerts the police, especially the victim, that they are nearby. This simple device could stop a lot of repeat occurrences and document harassment. No longer would a victim have to say, "He was standing in my backyard," and have the police arrive 30 minutes later. The GPS would document the stalker's location at all times.

It is important to remember that not all stalkers are afraid of the police or going to jail. They have a goal in their mind, and nothing will stop them from achieving it. You must use every resource to stop them. Remember to think like a stalker. Where would you stand to watch your house? Place a camera there!

Here is another one:

T.E.C.H.

T – Technology

E – Ever

C – Changing

H – Headache

Technology is always changing; you will win if you can be ahead of the game. If, for instance, your stalker is only tracking your phone location, get a second phone and don't back it up. Take the original phone and give it to your friend who is vacationing in Key West. This may provide a week of relief for you.

After finding a GPS device for the fifth time on her vehicle, we did this same ploy with a client. We placed the device on the car of a friend moving cross-country. When they arrived at their location, they placed it on the moving truck as the movers wanted to help and were headed south. We caught him placing a sixth GPS device on her car at her employer a few months later. The camera she parked under caught him in the act for the first time.

With today's technology, you should be able to look at the entire outside and inside of your residence via cameras and an app before you arrive home. You should be able to control turning lights on and off, giving the illusion you are home. Remember the movie *Home Alone*? Simple tactics like leaving the television on while you're not home can have someone waste a lot of time watching your house. While you film them, drive past to get a video of them and give the police enough time to catch them on location.

Technology can be an advantage for the stalker since more than twice as many victims are stalked using a form of technology: tracking your vehicle with GPS, spamming your email and social media, posting threats in message threads, using malware on your computer, and monitoring your cell phone are all problems we frequently assist with. The various cell phone monitoring brands of software are known as Stalkerware and can be tough to detect.

Some possible solutions:

GPS – Have a mechanic search your vehicle and have law enforcement remove the device

Email – Ignore, don't block them, as you will need proof of harassment

Social media – Same as above

Threats on threads – Set up Google Alerts to be aware when your name shows up, then contact the administrator

Malware – Get a good anti-virus or computer expert

Cell phone Stalkerware – Run a cell phone antivirus program, or factory reset the phone

Since Stalkerware has become a growing problem, you'll want to use a third party to remove it and document that it was there. How did the Stalkerware get there in the first place? The stalker likely had access to your phone, sent you a message link, or had your computer upload it. What can these apps reveal? They can show your location, calls, photos, emails, browsing history, and text messages. Some can even make the camera live, take photos, record, and send messages from your phone. Imagine your ex showing the court a text from you threatening to kill them!

This is a good time to remind you to have your cell phone screen locked at all times and not open for anyone to use! Having the inconvenience of a password or face scan is worth it.

Don't let anyone take your feeling of safety from you. Get educated about the technology you are using!

CHAPTER SIXTEEN

HOW TO STOP THE STALKING

"Nothing so needs reforming as other people's habits."

- *Mark Twain*

Out of sight, out of mind. Often, when a female who has been told to be nice her whole life ends a relationship with a guy, she is confusing in her communication. A nice message is often lost in translation, and the man hears what he wants to hear. As stated earlier, it is best to be direct and communicate that the relationship is over since our movies seem to promote persistence wins. If she says, "I'm not ready for a relationship," she is telling a stalker to wait until she is. No means no. People need to be truthful and direct when breaking up. In the case of celebrities, when meeting a fan, be nice but not overly nice. If they think they are special, this can be a problem later.

When I am asked the simplest way to make the harassment stop, I say, "Stop <u>ALL</u> communication." Let them go months without hearing from you. Outside of mental illness, they will likely focus on someone else. Since many stalkers had bad childhoods and fear rejection, they are looking for someone to possess that will never leave them. And note that "never leave them" may mean by murder-suicide.

Use the form we provided to help you document your case. You'll find that a restraining order is good for getting the legal process moving, but don't get complacent and think you are safer. Remember, the police don't wear paper-bulletproof vests? Many dead women are found with restraining orders on them. And remember, you are not alone. You have friends and family that seek your best interests and want you safe. I have listed examples in this book and advice on how a stalker gets information and how to stop it.

SAFETY TRIVIA

Let's play a safety from stalkers trivia game:

How do I?

- How do I own a house that's not in my name? Answer: <u>A trust</u>

- How can I drive a car that the plate does not come back to me? Answer: <u>Trade cars with a friend</u>

- How can I hide where I am? Answer: <u>Post false information</u>

- How can I call and text without them knowing my number? Answer: <u>A phone number app</u>

- How can I email and not be traced by the average person? Answer: <u>By using a VPN (a virtual private network)</u>

- How can I avoid being followed in my vehicle? Answer: <u>Change your daily driving routes and times</u>

- How can I avoid them knowing where I work? Answer: <u>Don't post it on social media</u>

- How can I avoid them knowing so much personal information? Answer: <u>Stop living out loud on social media</u>

- How can I stop data sites from posting my personal information? Answer: <u>Contact them and request to be removed</u>

- How can I confuse the addresses posted for me? Answer: <u>Change your credit card addresses to physical bank locations in other states</u>

- How can I stop the post office from my forwarding address be obtained? Answer: <u>Have your mail sent to a UPS store</u>

- How do I file a restraining order? Answer: <u>Contact your local police department</u>

- How do I obtain an address that will keep me hidden? Answer: <u>Use a mailing business that will scan your mail and email it to you</u>

THINK LIKE A STALKER AND STOP THEM

I recommend that stalked clients write a "Safety Story Sheet." On this sheet, they write their story on where they allegedly moved, where they are allegedly working, etc. They then share with trusted friends, neighbors, and family to have them maintain a consistent story. Make certain they understand that your safety is at risk. Taking precautions like address confusion via credit card addresses and asking your utility companies not to share information about you is a good move. A prepaid cell phone is tough to track, and a second-line app number is smart.

Think of something you are obsessed with. What lengths would you go to get that concert ticket or rare collectible. Stalkers make you their obsession and often don't care about their own well-being or the consequences of obtaining you. Some have the attitude that if they can't have you, no one will. You are important, and the world is a better place with you in it. Your life is worth the fight. Learn a martial art, get your gun-carry permit, and have an escape plan.

People hire me to locate them and then ask how hard it is. I think it is a valuable exercise, as I can tell them where they went wrong and how to fix it.

These days of living out loud on social media make stalking easier than ever. Reddit and TikTok were used in a recent case to determine which hotel a celebrity was staying in and then shared for all to see.

Finally, remember that stopping ALL CONTACT can frequently make the person get the message and go away. Remember the example that if someone calls you 85 times and you respond on the 86th, you are telling them it takes 86 times to reach you. Let them call you one thousand times with absolutely no response. Police sometimes react to domestic violence and stalking cases like they don't care. This is because they have seen women call for help only to take the abuser back time and time again. Stopping all contact literally means stopping all contact via phone, email, social media, text, and meetings. It is the best and cheapest way to an end. When you need help, do not delay telling friends and family about your issue. They are there for you and can help you with a plan of action. Use our form, get the help you need, and know you are not alone.

THINK LIKE A STALKER AND STOP THEM

THE END

Connect with Michael Kenney Private Investigator

Twitter.com/MichaelKenneyPI

NOTES

Made in United States
Orlando, FL
03 January 2024